Thomas Hardy's Novels: A Feminist Perspective

Thomas Hardy's Novels: A Feminist Perspective

Isam M. Shihada

PRESTIGE

Published by

PRESTIGE BOOKS

3/28, East Patel Nagar

New Delhi 110 008

e-mail: prestigebooks@greatindian.com

ISBN: 81-7551-095-1

Composed by Vivek Mathur, Delhi 110 006 Ph. 3981867

Printed at Chaman Offset Press, New Delhi 110 002

Contents

Preface

The aim of this study is to examine the feminist aspects of Thomas Hardy's major novels. The intention here is to study the contribution made by Hardy to the development and emergence of the modern woman.

During the Victorian age, a number of male novelists began writing about women, offering fine examples of varied treatment of feminist aspects. Among these novelists, Thomas Hardy occupies an important place. It is, therefore, of great interest and value to examine the treatment of this subject in the major works of Thomas Hardy. In a certain sense, Hardy could be considered a precursor of the feminist movement. This is an area in which considerable work has been done but it still offers immense scope for further study. It is interesting to know that the basic elements of feminism are found in Thomas Hardy's major novels which will be the focus of this study.

Hardy established himself as a distinguished novelist of the nineteenth century. Through his works of fiction, he involved himself in projecting his image of men and women in a particular social context which he portrayed. He was highly critical of the place and treatment of women in the Victorian society. His sympathies went out to the women in the Victorian age and the unequal treatment given to them due to the unjust marriage laws. He worked tirelessly in order to change the male-dominated society and to bring about the desired changes for the mutual benefit of women as well as men.

The Victorian society of the nineteenth century was a rigid and uncompromising one towards women. The laws governing the social and marital affairs were all male-oriented and deeply entrenched in their implementation and adherence. It was in this atmosphere that Hardy took up the onus on himself, of projecting the various issues with a hope of finding a solution. Hardy pointed out the ills of the contemporary society and presented the ways of solving them. Thus, feminism originated from the need for women to have a choice about the kind of life they wished to lead. Feminists demand that women should be treated as autonomous individuals and not as passive objects of men's fancy; that women should not be considered inferior to men; that equal attention and opportunities should be given to women for education and employment for their economic independence. In the Victorian society, man was placed as superior to woman and he refused to accept woman as a companion on equal terms. Thus, the need for the emancipation of women arose. Mary Wollstonecraft, J.S. Mill, Simone De Beauvoir and Andrea Dworkin championed the feminist movement for liberation of women.

Hardy was successful in projecting women's helpless situation by defying the well-entrenched social customs. His role is one of a pioneer showing the new emerging women the way to their emancipation from the strictly conventional, uncaring and unsympathetic society. In his novels, we come across women who are passive and vain as well as women who are ambitious and independent and do not conform to the rigid moral codes and social systems.

Since love has by no means the same meaning for both the sexes, Hardy points out that it becomes the cause for serious misunderstandings that separate them. For a woman, love is not only devotion but a total surrendering of body and soul without any reservation. Enclosed in her own sphere, under male domination, love becomes one of the means to assert her worth. Hence, we find that women are enchanted by man's virility, wealth, distinction of manners and social status.

The organization of the book is as follows. Chapter One is a brief sketch of Thomas Hardy's life, and his works. It makes a thematic analysis of all his fourteen novels and the factors that contributed to his development as a feminist writer.

Chapter Two covers the various approaches to feminism—liberal, Marxist, radical, social, existentialist and post-modern. Each one of these is only a partial answer to the woman's question. It is fascinating to see how these approaches explore the ways in which women have been oppressed and find solutions for their problems. It considers Hardy as a liberal feminist as he has dealt extensively with liberal issues like conventionality in marriage, unequal divorce laws, the inadequate facilities for women's education and mistreatment of women by men. However, if Hardy's feminism is to be understood in the right perspective, it must be seen in relation to the contemporary feminist theories.

Chapter Three stresses the point that marriage is never isolated from social status and that construes Fancy Day's hesitation in making up her mind about her suitors—Maybold, Dick and Shiner in *Under the Greenwood Tree*. It is not only a matter of her choice of a future husband but also the class of society which she wishes to join. The chapter discusses Hardy's vehement enthusiasm for a woman like Fancy Day who defied the conventional norms of the Victorian period by thinking for herself and charting her own destiny. It is her education that helped her to lead the kind of life she wanted and that conforms to the feminist ideals that education and employment are basic elements needed for women in order to be independent.

Chapter Four deals with *Far from the Madding Crowd*, a story of Bathsheba Everdene who is better educated and occupies a higher social position. Hardy is full of praise for her since she is a free thinking and unconventional woman. She abhors male domination. As she says, "I hate to be thought men's property in that way, though possibly I shall be had some day." (37) This is in conformity with the feminist argument that women should not be treated as sexual objects. Hardy depicts Bathsheba as a woman who is strongly individualized and capable of charting her own life. Bathsheba's marriage failed partly due to her vanity and Troy's infidelity and his lack of understanding that women are human beings with values and rights of their own.

Chapter Five deals with *The Return of the Native* which is about Eustacia Vye, a type of woman who defies restrictions and prefers to live a free life far away from Egdon Heath. She asserts her individuality by refusing to conform to the conventional norms and her fight for her self-respect makes her distinct. Eustacia Vye is a contrast to Thomasin Yeobright who is a dependent woman and who makes no extravagant demands on life but is content to be a mother and wife, the typical Victorian woman who accepts the superiority of men and social traditions in spite of her husband's infidelity. This chapter deals with Hardy's condemnation of such passivity which can be justified as a major obstacle in the liberation of women.

Chapter Six deals with *The Mayor of Casterbridge* which is a continuation of the theme of treating women as inessential beings. Michael Henchard sells his wife for five guineas and proves the point that man does not consider his wife as someone equal to him and worthy. No law seems to have been in existence to prevent such injustice done to women. We also find that the role of the furmity woman is to see that crimes like Henchard's should not be allowed to go unpunished. This chapter highlights Susan's simplicity and passivity as causes of her suffering. In contrast Elizabeth-Jane is depicted as an intelligent, well-informed stable young woman capable of managing her affairs. Lucetta is a woman who leads an unconventional life, disapproved by society and therefore is crushed out of existence. This chapter highlights Hardy's fight for his heroines and their rights. Hardy condemns the male supremacy exercised by Henchard when he takes advantage of Susan's simplicity. He also condemns the docile nature of Susan and her attitude towards her husband as a breakdown of male superiority against the female endurance.

Chapter Seven deals with *The Woodlanders* which is an account of Grace Melbury. She becomes a victim of her own father's unreasonable ambition to obtain a higher social status through her marriage. He exerts pressure on his daughter to marry a young and ambitious man Dr. Fitzpiers. In total obedience, Grace marries Dr. Fitzpiers but soon discovers his extramarital affairs with other women which amount to adultery and desertion. In this chapter, an attempt has been made to highlight the unequal divorce laws. Grace pleads for divorce but she is not granted the right to break the marriage bond citing that Dr. Fitzpiers's treatment of her was not harsh enough to break the marriage. Thus, she is resigned to live the rest of her life with a man for whom she has no love or respect. Marty South, a young woman with considerable abilities, is unable to realize her ambitions due to her passivity and conventional upbringing. We also see Hardy's attitude towards women; if they are brought up the same way as men are, they are bound to be successful.

Chapter Eight projects *Tess of the D'Urbervilles* as a story of Tess Durbyfield who is a victim of rape by Alec D'Urbervilles for whom she worked. Hardy blames the social and religious establishments for Tess's sufferings. He also attacks the double moral standards of the Victorian age. Through Angel's characterization, Hardy illustrates that life-denying ideas are extremely destructive. An attempt has been made to show Tess's meekness and the endurance in her love for Angel Clare evoke bitter emotions and sympathy as she realizes that she was mistaken in accepting Clare's estimate of her.

Chapter Nine, *Jude the Obscure*, is about Jude Fawley, an ambitious young man who was trapped between two distinctly contrasting women Arabella Donn and Sue Bridehead. It is mainly about the shattered ideas of its two major characters—Jude Fawley and Sue Bridehead—who defied the stiff Victorian moral codes regarding the conventional marriage laws. Hardy advocates that women should have the right to exercise their will in choosing their life partners and in expressing their feelings. The chapter highlights Hardy's views on marriage that it should be based on mutual understanding, trust and love. Hardy stresses that man is not entitled to force any woman, even his wife, to live with him. For him, marriage is not a physical union but a union based on harmony, love and understanding.

The concluding chapter highlights Hardy's contribution to

women's liberation and his untiring efforts to educate men and women about the need to create a healthy society in which women are given due respect and privileges on equal terms. Hardy tried to destroy what he felt was a false order and advocated changes in laws concerning marriage, divorce and maltreatment of women by men. Hardy proves that a human being's longing for happiness is far more important than the social conventions and psychological inhibitions which only suppress and thwart them.

I cannot close these prefatory remarks without expressing my deep sense of gratitude to Dr. N.M. Aston, Reader and Head, Department of English, Nowrosjee Wadia College, Pune for his scholarly comments and invaluable suggestions that I received from time to time during the course of writing this book. I wish to acknowledge the help and co-operation I received from numerous friends, prominent among them being Shradha Pandhanani, Azzam Khalaf, Dr. Firas Rawashdh, Khalid Abu Zayed, Dimple Vaswani, Sonia Mendonca, Alina Runcan, Ruba Yasin, Muneer Rayan and Yousef Yousef, and many others whose names have not been mentioned here.

I dedicate this work, with sincere regards and gratitude, to my loving parents, my brothers and sisters for their support, moral as well as financial, towards bringing out this book.

Chapter One

Introduction

Thomas Hardy was born in Old Dorset Stock at Higher Bockhampton, a hamlet in the parish of Stinsford near Dorchester on 2 June 1840. His forefathers were masons who undertook small construction jobs. Hardy inherited their creative spirit and their determination to do the job at their best. His father, Senior Thomas Hardy, was a master-mason who also sang at weddings. Hardy developed love for music while accompanying his father on various occasions. The involvement of his family in Stinsford Church choir figures prominently in his novel, *Under the Greenwood Tree.*

There is evidence to show that Hardy's character was shaped, to a large extent, under the powerful influence and the dynamic guidance of his mother Jemima, a stimulating woman with an unusual ability and judgment of her own. She was instrumental in making Hardy read the works of John Dryden and Dr. Samuel Johnson when he was just ten years old. There existed a strong bond between mother and son and Hardy inherited much of her character, her interest in people, her love for a good story and her view that life has buffets as well as rewards to offer. Hardy's obvious interest in the manner women were treated in his time and his sympathy for them as depicted in the major works can be the outcome, to some extent, of his close association with his mother.

In 1850, Hardy was sent to Dorchester British School, three miles away from Bockhampton. His thorough knowledge of Dorset, its history and topography was acquired during his daily walk to the school. His major novels are full of minute descriptions of the recollections from his childhood memories.

In Dorchester, there was much for a keen-sighted child to observe. Public executions were still carried out in full view, outside the massive red-brick jail and Hardy had the occasion to witness one of them. It was on 9 August 1856 that Martha Browne was executed on the charge of murdering her husband. Though Hardy was just sixteen years old, he was convinced of the fact that Martha Browne was innocent. This incident accounts for Tess being hanged in *Tess of the D'Urbervilles*.

Hardy's full-time scholastic education ended in July 1856. Although it had provided him with an education far better than anyone belonging to his class, he didn't possess the requisite proficiency in the classics to enter the university. Hence he suffered from inferiority complex which found literary expression in his novel, *Jude the Obscure*, where Jude was advised by the master of Biblioll College to remain in his own sphere.

It was at this stage of his life that his mother influenced him to be an apprentice to an architect, Mr. John Hicks of Dorchester. Hicks recognized Hardy as a promising student and readily agreed to accept him on a lower premium than usual. The choice of architecture as an occupation can be seen as another decisive step towards his preparation to become a writer. Hardy was under the efficient training of Mr. Hicks who did leave him enough time to pursue his other studies and interests.

At Hicks's office, Hardy found himself among fellow-pupils whose discussions were both challenging and stimulating. One of the pupils, Henry Barstow, was very enthusiastic about the classics. Barstow and Hardy sharpened their intelligence through lengthy discussions based on various subjects such as infant-baptism which later found a place in *Tess of the D'Urbervilles* where Tess baptized her son as 'Sorrow' at home. However, these discussions entailed lengthy study of the Greek New Testament and that helped Hardy in acquiring a profound and comprehensive knowledge of the Bible. Timothy Hands observes: "The words Hardy uses are greatly affected by his religious past and there were more than six hundred biblical allusions in the fourteen published novels." (1989: 14) F.B. Pinion also remarks: "No other book, not even the works of Shakespeare, informed the thought and character of Hardy as much as the Bible." (1968:14)

Hardy met William Barnes, a poet who lived near Hicks's office. Barnes taught Hardy the usage of English language and poetic techniques which helped him in his career as a novelist and as a poet later on.

Hardy's career as an architect played a vital role in shaping his novels. The leading characters in his novels, *Desperate Remedies*, *A Pair of Blue Eyes* and *A Laodicean* are architects. While describing Weatherbury Church in *Far from the Madding Crowd* he uses considerable imaginative force. The buildings fascinated him a lot. His major novels are treated with the care and attention that a skilled architect would give to a pet project. *The Mayor of Casterbridge* stands out as a fine example of his achievement in this respect and the internal divisions of his novels under headings such as 'Books' and 'Phases' bring out his skill of being an architect.

The years between 1856 and 1862 were of immense importance to Hardy's mental and cultural growth. Millgate writes that much of Hardy's reading "was done between five and eight in the morning before he left home for the office." (1984:32) It can be said that Hardy's zeal for self-education impelled him to read extensively. He had the full support of his mother whose hold was so strong that theirs was a close knit family with four children. Mary followed Thomas Hardy in 1841 and after a gap of ten years, Henry was born in 1851 and Katherine in 1856. Hardy was very close to Mary and there was a strong bond of affection and understanding between them. Mary was trained as a school teacher at Salisbury Training College and Hardy drew upon her knowledge and experience to provide material for his novel *Jude the Obscure*.

Another major influence on Hardy's mental and spiritual development was Horace Moule. Moule was a freelance essayist and a reviewer. They became friends in 1854 and Moule presented Hardy a copy of Jabez Hogg's *Elements of Experi-*

mental and Natural Philosophy.

Moule also guided Hardy's reading and sympathized with his aspiration of becoming an author. It might have been Moule who made Hardy aware of the geological discoveries which challenged the truth of some passages of the Old Testament. They also discussed Darwin's *The Origin of Species* (1859) which shattered Hardy's religious beliefs. A dispute between Horace and his father in which Horace was rebuked for buying theologically unacceptable books of that time, was used by Hardy for the scene in *Tess of the D'Urbervilles* where Angel Clare is rebuked in a similar manner by his father. This may account for the lack of understanding between parents and their children which figured prominently in *The Woodlanders*, *Tess of the D'Urbervilles*, and *The Return of the Native*.

However, the tension between the father and the son must have contributed to Moule's taking to alcoholism. Hardy would certainly have known the other side of Moule's character and the outbursts of Jude may owe something to his observation of Moule's lapses. Moule suffered periods of intense melancholy due to a broken relationship with an anonymous woman and from a feeling of frustration that it would not be possible for him to become a famous essayist. Angel Clare in *Tess of the D'Urbervilles* and Henry Knight in *A Pair of Blue Eyes* were drawn upon Horace Moule's character, especially in their conventional attitudes towards women and their loss of religious faith. Horace Moule's suicide in 1873 had a great effect on Hardy.

In 1860, Hardy completed his architectural training but he continued to work for Hicks as a paid assistant, earning fifteen shillings a week. London had been brought much closer by the railway and a new element of mobility manifested itself in the lives of Dorset's inhabitants. At the age of twenty-two, Hardy went to London to advance his architectural and literary ambitions. He joined the staff of a flourishing young architect named Arthur Blomfield, a man of great insight and kindness. In his spare time, Hardy read widely, attended lectures and went to concerts and galleries. The writings of Huxley and the discussions in periodicals such as *The Saturday Review* to which Moule had contributed, made a deep impression on Hardy.

In his novels, Hardy frequently draws upon his knowledge of art by using paintings as images that enrich description and add an extra dimension to his writings. In *Far from the Madding Crowd*, the description of Gabriel Oak standing with a lamp by his hut can be taken as a visual echo of Holman Hunt's painting 'The Light of the World' in which Christ stands besides a hut with a lantern. However, it was music, architecture, and art which contributed greatly towards developing Hardy's power of characterization.

While in London between 1862 and 1867, Hardy began to think seriously of becoming a writer. He had written some verse while living in Dorchester but he did not take it seriously at all. Although Hardy was better known as a novelist, his first wish was to be a poet. He returned to writing poetry after the harsh criticism which *Jude the Obscure* and his defence of women's rights received.

It is believed that Hardy's close relationship with his mother Jemima and the writings of J.S. Mill, especially *The Subjection of Women* (1869) were particularly responsible for his defence of women's rights in his major novels. He explored widely controversial issues of that period like the conventionality of marriage, the oppression and maltreatment of women by men, unfair divorce laws and the credibility of social and religious institutions. Hardy's feminist views began to appear gradually and slowly in his major novels due to the pressure by publishers in order to satisfy the tastes of Victorian readers.

In July 1912, Hardy's wife, Emma Gifford, died after a brief illness. Her death affected Hardy a lot and he composed some very good elegies thereafter. There is no doubt that some of her pride is reflected in the character of some of his heroines. After his wife's death, Hardy took the help of Florence Dugdale, a close family friend. Florence's devotion to and understanding of Hardy's needs, drew Hardy close to her. In February 1914, they were married. Hardy wrote poetry until the end of 1927 when his health started deteriorating. His last poem was "Winter Words" which he had already revised and got ready for publication. On 11 January 1928, Hardy passed away. He was buried in Westminster Abbey in the presence of a large gathering.

During the eighty-eight years of his life, Hardy published fourteen novels, four volumes of short stories, eight volumes of verse and an epic drama, *The Dynasts.* Hardy classified his works for the Wessex edition 1912 as Novels of Character and Environment: *Under the Greenwood Tree* (1872), *Far From the Madding Crowd* (1874), *The Return of the Native* (1878), *The Mayor of Casterbridge* (1886), *The Woodlanders* (1887), *Tess of the D'Urbervilles* (1891), *Jude the Obscure* (1895); Novels of Romances and Fantasies: *A Pair of Blue Eyes* (1873), *The Trumpet-Major* (1880), *Two on a Tower* (1882), *A Group of Noble Dames* (1891), *The Well-Beloved* (1897); Novels of Ingenuity: *Desperate Remedies* (1871), *The Hand of Ethelberta* (1876), *A Laodicean* (1881), *A Changed Man* (stories) (1913); Poetry: *The Dynasts* (1903), *Wessex Poems* (1898), *Poems of the Past and the Present* (1901), *Times of the Past and the Present* (1909), *Satires of Circumstances* (1914), *Moments of Vision* (1917), *Late Lyrics and Earlier* (1922), *Human Shows* (1925), *Winter Words* (1928).

Of all genres of literature, fiction in particular is woven around the relationship between men and women, the family and the society at large and portrays the interaction between the characters. Characterization, therefore, becomes the primary concern of the novelist. It also compels the novelist to project the images of men and women in a particular social context.

In the 1860s Hardy had written a substantial amount of verse at the outset of his career but it had been indifferently received. The publication of his epic-drama, *The Dynasts*, brought him recognition as a poet. But in the next twenty years, his creative efforts went into writing novels and short stories.

Hardy's novels include some major fiction as well as some minor ones. When his major novels such as *Tess of the D'Urbervilles* (1891) and *Jude the Obscure* were published, they were immediately branded "immoral" and "obscene." Today we are moved by Hardy's wonderful stories and magnificent understanding of human passion and desire.

We can applaud Hardy's frank portrayal of the relationships between men and women, irrespective of their social position. Besides, his novels offer a rich variety of reading experience with equally varied themes pertaining to the simple man-woman relationship in its countless manifestations which shall be critically, though briefly, examined in this chapter.

In spite of the human richness and professional confidence of the major novels, Hardy's minor novels should not be ignored since they also play a significant part in the dynamic process of the development of Hardy's fiction, each of them contributing something to our understanding of Thomas Hardy and his work as a whole.

Hardy's first novel, *Desperate Remedies*, has a lively assortment of ingredients: a murder, a dramatic fire, a suicide and extensive allusions. The tone of the novel varies from comedy to tragedy and from the flippant to the gruesome. But the total fusion of these separate elements is scarcely possible and Hardy's handling of the material is tentative. The weakness of the work is shrewdly concealed in its apt classification as a Novel of Ingenuity.

In *Desperate Remedies*, physical interest is predominant and an intense psychological pressure operates not far below the surface. The constant sexual pressure is unusual in kind and intensity, exceptional even in a sensational novel. The most remarkable feature of the novel is the relationship between the heroine Cytherea and the formidable and wealthy Miss Aldclyffe, her employer. The early stages of their encounter have a sensual directness. Hardy lays emphasis on what he declares to be the maternal nature of Miss Aldclyffe's passionate behaviour.

Miss Aldclyffe describes herself as an ill-tempered woman, a foolish and a wicked old sinner. She is shown as a victim of severe emotional repressions and her outburst as classical instance of frustrated sexuality.

Cytherea's inner life is made more prominent from the beginning and she enjoys a complexity denied to the conventional heroine. She is Hardy's first flirt, vain enough to be pleased with her beauty. Although Cytherea is the pivotal character, the dominating one is Aeneas Manston, the evil genius of the story. He is a victim of social misfortune and Miss Aldclyffe's son from an illegal relationship. Miss Aldclyffe encourages Manston to marry Cytherea but the plan fails when it is discovered that Manston had killed and buried his first wife. The novel ends with the happy union of Cytherea and Edward Springrove. There is evidence of Hardy showing his sentiments on matters he cared about—pressures from social institutions, the marriage contract and social stratification.

In *Under the Greenwood Tree*, the heroine, Fancy Day, is loved by Dick Dewy, the first in the line of honest, open-hearted countrymen whose lack of guile makes them easy victims of the calculating and faithless women. Dick is considered a less eligible suitor for Fancy because he is the son of a farmer. Dick looks forward to becoming the manager of his father's business. Fancy's social position is between the Dewys and Maybold. She is a qualified school mistress and her father, a game-keeper. Maybold and Shiner have sexual interest in Fancy Day.

Fancy's vocation is to marry someone, something reinforced by her temperament and upbringing. Whom she marries is to be determined by considerations other than love and this is made clear in Dick's conversation with her snobbish father who sees marriage as a means of rising in the world. Fancy shares her father's susceptibility to external good breeding and his relative indifference to love. Throughout their relationship, Dick is made painfully conscious that she cares less about him than about herself. She accepts parson Maybold who is much above her socially. In contrast to Dick's warm and undivided love for her, she has no deep emotions and allows herself to be attracted by one man and then by another in proportion to how much they feed her vanity.

In Hardy's novels, marriage is never isolated from social status and that construes Fancy Day's hesitation among Maybold, Dick and Shiner. In other words, it is not only a matter of whom she prefers, but also which group she wants to join.

Hardy has shown his vehement enthusiasm for women like Fancy Day who defied the conventional norms of the Victorian age by thinking for herself and choosing what is suitable for her. Probably her education helped her to lead the kind of life she wanted and that conforms to the feminist ideals that education and work are the basic elements needed to shed the halo of dependence and to provide an escape from man's superiority. The novel ends in an ironic note as Fancy Day, finally has to accept Dick Dewy. D.H. Lawrence observes: "Fancy, the little school mistress returns to Dick, renounces imagination and settles down to steady, solid, physically married life. But Fancy will carry in her heart all her life many unopened buds that will die unflowered." (1985:22)

A Pair of Blue Eyes is a Victorian novel concerned with time, class, men and women whose sexual feelings are deeply constrained by convention. Hardy classified the novel among "Romances and Fantasies" as if to suggest its visionary nature.

In *A Pair of Blue Eyes*, Elfride sets off a train of disappointments and regrets by what seem to be harmless deceits. She deceives Felix Jethway into believing that she loves him. He allows his mother to believe that Elfride has jilted him. Hence, Mrs. Jethway develops deep hatred for Elfride.

Another web of deceit begins with Stephen Smith who persuades Elfride to elope with him. When the elopement ends in a hasty withdrawal, Elfride deceives her father and her next suitor, Henry Knight, by suppressing uncomfortable facts. When Stephen Smith returns and by chance meets Elfride with Knight to whom she is now engaged, he falls in with the general air of deception and doesn't permit his own previous engagement to Elfride become known to Knight.

Though Elfride has not committed any sin, she is caught in the toils of deception from a general concern with keeping up of appearances. She wanted to tell Henry Knight the truth but the intense fear which accompanies intense love in young women was very strong. While she hesitates, Knight inexorably raises the stakes and says: "Elfride, there is one thing I do love to see in a woman that is, a soul truthful and clear as heaven's light." (217)

Elfride conceals the details of her past life from Knight just as she had from Stephen. The burden of confession accumulates to her disadvantage as she now has two former sweethearts to reveal to the astonished Knight. Elfride marries the widowed Lord Luxellian. Shortly, she dies in pregnancy. When Knight and Stephen travel by the same train that carries Elfride's coffin from London to Cornwall, it becomes to them a journey of reconciliation with Elfride. The denouement at their journey's end closes the story on an unexpected note of tragic comedy.

In the process, Hardy's vision of a world that is socially inequitable is brought to light and the social divisions and snobbery furnish an urgent theme. Hardy's indignation at the lowering of a master-mason's profession is evident. Parson Swancourt who is socially a snob, helped in spoiling the happiness of Elfride and Stephen. At the same time, to satisfy his own pretensions, he is prepared to marry money in the unbeguiling form of Charlotte Troyton. Stephen's mother while resenting Swancourt's snobbery, ironically displays her own by telling her son.

> She is not a bit too high for you, or you too low for her. See how careful I am to keep myself up. I am sure I never stop for more than a minute together to talk to any journey-men people; and I never invite anybody to our party of Christmas who are not in business for themselves. (69)

Class division is the barrier that the young architect cannot surmount, and it is a problem exacerbated by the urban community. Elfride is the first heroine to realize her tragic potential. She is a flirt who readily plays the role of 'La Belle Dame Sans Merci.' She convicts herself of the superficiality of which Hardy disapproves in women. Her fault lies not in her action but in her inaction. Her indecision is the main reason for her tragedy. She keeps Knight in dark about Jethway and her marriage appointment with Stephen. So, she cannot escape the responsibility for her fecklessness. Eventually, the force of her inaction leads to her tragedy but Knight's pompous indignation and contempt make the readers show full sympathy for Elfride. Knight's jealousy and selfishness also contribute to Elfride's tragedy.

Knight is an intriguing compound of honesty, intelligence, naivety and sexual peculiarity. The peculiar nature of perfection that he seeks, tends to be the result of his unusual lack of experience with women. Even in the context of Victorian inhibitions, it is odd that he attained the age of thirty-two without kissing any woman other than his mother and this implies a reserve of repressed sexuality within him. Knight is the first helpless idealist in Hardy's novels. These people, Hardy suggests with profound sympathy for them, are not fit for the world. Repression is a condition that is pointed out many times in his novels. However, Elfride, a poor victim of passion, is not strong enough to overthrow the most repressive conventional ideas.

In *Far from the Madding Crowd*, we find three men of different temperaments aspiring for Bathsheba's hand: Gabriel Oak, the shepherd, who is a combination of goodness and strength, Troy a traditional soldier who does not belong to the rural community and does not share its values and manners and farmer Boldwood whose feelings drive him to obsession, crime and madness. *Far from the Madding Crowd* sealed Hardy's commitment to Wessex as the theatre of his imagination. It was in the pages of the novel that the name of the old Saxon Kingdom began to exchange its historical and antiquarian associations for the new meaning that Hardy has given it.

Far from the Madding Crowd is about marriage, adultery and death, Bathsheba Everdene is a fine creation and perhaps the most normal and natural of Hardy's heroines. Hardy says, "There was a bright air and manner about her now, by which she seemed to imply that the desirability of her existence couldn't be questioned." (26)

Her vanity is her vulnerable point on which the whole action hinges. It is a theme that Hardy was much engaged with. Hardy has shown his praise of Bathsheba's drift from conventionality and alluded largely to her being a free thinking and non-conformist woman. Bathsheba feels initiated by Oak when he himself feels to be receiving a signal of some sort. "I hate to be thought men's property in that way, though possibly I shall be had someday." (37) That conforms to feminist's argument that women shouldn't be treated as sexual objects. Bathsheba's unwise marriage failed due to Troy's infidelity and partly due to her own vanity. Troy's lack of understanding that a woman is a human being with values and rights may be responsible for his affair with Fanny Robin who died in pregnancy in one of the workshops of Casterbridge. Hardy asserts that love for Bathsheba, as for man, will become a source of life and not of moral danger. Bathsheba's marriage with Oak is finally a success due to Oak's devotion to her and his treating her as an equal.

Bathsheba's sin can be attributed to her abasement before a pleasure-seeking man interested only in conquest. But Troy's affection and tenderness are committed elsewhere—to one of Bathsheba's servants, a humble and artless Fanny Robin. In comparison with Hardy's major feminine portraits, Fanny is little more than a conventionally stylized version of the betrayed maid. Dying at child birth in Casterbridge workhouse, Fanny exudes Hardy's compassion to produce some of the most powerful passages he had ever written. However, the novel ends with a happy union between the loyal and useful Oak and Bathsheba.

The Hand of Ethelberta (1876) is an outcry against unfair privilege, social advantage, urban pretensions, hypocrisy and foolish aspirations. It is also a vigorous protest against all sorts of repressions in London. The upper classes suppress emotions, sincerity and integrity and deprive the lower classes of their rightful dignity.

Ethelberta is the most worldly and ambitious of all Hardy's heroines. She gets married to Lord Mountclere but manages to suppress her emotions and healthy sexuality, in pursuit of a much less wholesome ideal, the acquisition of social rank, status and wealth. When she contemplates marriage with Mountclere, she looks for ethical and financial support for her family. She wants to involve the happiness of all concerned rather than that of her own. The socio-economic basis of her assumption is false because her family neither needs nor wishes to be provided for through such a materialistic compromise.

In the end, Ethelberta who becomes a victim of her own foolish compromise is alienated from her family. She is unable to sleep because she sees battalions of lovers denouncing her with the finger of ridicule. She is full of contradictions that make her real.

In this novel, the contrast between the countryside and town is sustained throughout and made more explicit than in any other of the Wessex novels. Since the novel is ironic, the ending is vital. The comic is realized but Hardy does not investigate the deeper implications of the conclusion. However, the novel has to be understood and read as a comedy of manners.

The Return of the Native carries Hardy's sense of dramatic qualities. Under the full play of Hardy's imagination, the Heath transcends its inanimate character and acquires human attributes. Hardy says in this regard: "As with some persons who have long lived apart, solitude seemed to look out of its countenance. It had a lonely face, suggesting tragical possibilities." (5)

In the novel we find changing relationships among the characters. At the outset, Eustacia Vye and Wildeve have a curious and secret cold romance which terminates when Wildeve marries Thomasin and Eustacia pairs up with Clym. Eustacia dreams of the day, when as Clym's wife, she would be passing her days in a gay world. But Clym renounces all that Paris and the diamond trade symbolize. He wants to settle down at Egdon Heath as a teacher of the underprivileged.

Eustacia Vye is the most sensational and volcanic of Hardy's heroines. Never did he use more startling exuberant phrases in his description than of hers. Hardy says, "Eustacia Vye was the raw material of divinity . . . she had the passions and instincts which make a model goddess, that is, those make not quite a model woman." (63)

To be loved to madness, such was Eustacia's great desire as it would drive away the eating loneliness of her days. More shrewdly, Hardy observes that she seemed to long for the abstraction called passionate love more than for any particular lover.

Her marriage with Clym is doomed from the outset. Her belief that she can persuade him to return to Paris turns out to be a pathetic delusion. Clym's determination to qualify as a teacher by intensive study is frustrated by his failing eye-sight. There is always danger around their already troubled married life, the possessive mother and Wildeve. Mrs. Yeobright's attitude to her future daughter-in-law is unequivocal. She condemns her as a lazy, dissatisfied and hussy woman. The threat from Wildeve is more erratic and fitful. Hardy describes Wildeve as a man "yearning for the difficult, to be weary of what offered to care for the remote, to dislike the near; it was Wildeve's nature always." (216)

If *A Pair of Blue Eyes* is about deception, *The Return of the Native* is about misunderstanding between men and women. Eustacia clings to the impossible belief that Clym will after all go to Paris and Clym considers her to be an ideal school matron.

Hardy depicts Thomasin as a dependent woman who makes no extravagant demands on life but is content to be a mother and wife, the type of Victorian woman who accepts the superiority of man and society. Wildeve resembles Troy in his infidelity to his wife Thomasin. The only thing that can rouse him to an emotional fever is to find Thomasin desired by someone else and that accounts for his mentality that women are objects to be possessed. Thomasin's reticence, dependence and conventionality are responsible for her misery and Hardy's condemnation of such passivity can be justified as he considered dependence to be a major obstacle on the road to freedom for women.

Eustacia Vye is a kind of woman who defies restrictions and needs to live a free life far away from the suffocating Egdon Heath. She asserts her independence and individuality by refusing to conform to the conventional mores. Treating a woman as an inessential being continues to be a prominent theme in all the major novels of Thomas Hardy.

The Trumpet Major is set in the Napoleonic era. Hardy's deliberate course of reading and research at the British Museum shows the admirable respect he had for historical precision as he never took such pains over the preparation for any other novel. As a departure from romance and adventure, this novel is an evocation of time and war and man's inhumanity to man. The shades of Napoleonic background are cast over the happenings at Overcome and Budmouth.

The action revolves around the miller and his mill. The noble rivalry between the two sons of Miller Loveday for the hand of Anne Garland is conducted as per the conventional rules of light romantic fiction. The central theme concerns the choice of a husband for Anne. The novel is a study of the emotional vicissitudes of two contrasting personalities, John and Bob. The steady virtues of honour, loyalty and patience go unrewarded while victory crowns the inconstant and less worthy Bob.

John Loveday is the spiritual successor of Springrove, Stephen Smith, Oak and Diggory Venn, the latest in a series of quiet and good men who engage Hardy's admiration. Anne's choice of the wrong man is entirely in character with the innocent and unsophisticated woman but it is equally true to life in more fundamental sense that the heart is ruled by more delicate impulses than objective reasons can supply. Just as Ethelberta had shown the emotional sterility by allowing reason to dominate passion, Anne's behaviour shows the exclusion of reason from her eventual decision.

As a heroine, occupying a central role, Anne Garland lacks the intelligence of Cytherea and Fancy Day. Of all heroines, Anne is the most colourless. Her personality does not develop through experience and the results of her fluctuating decisions leave no perceptible mark on her. However, we find Hardy critical of her general pride and dullness. Hardy reports here her shallow preference for a dashing presentment, a naval rank and a worthier stand. Her choice may be natural but her serious flaw is the extent of her perversity which amounts to callousness. The remaining characters are only functional and apart from Captain Hardy, psychologically unrealized.

A Laodicean is a fascinating exposition of Hardy's social beliefs and his concern about the aesthetic and cultural implications of social revolution. It has been written under the stress of physical incapacity due to his illness. It reflects the central problems of Victorian culture, class and the relationship of men and women through the love story of George Somerset and Paula Power. It is a feminist novel and its merits and demerits need to be measured in the context of the novels about women in the 1870s and 1880s. It contains more of the facts of Hardy's own life than anything else he had ever written. It was his illness that drove him to put in so much of himself in the novel.

Paula Power, the heroine of *A Laodicean*, is an educated woman but women's education was superficial, as feminists during the first half of the nineteenth century complained. During that time, women were trained only for courtship and marriage. Hence, we find that Paula's vocation is thrown into relief through her relationships with men. Paula's attitude to her sexuality is entirely free from frigidity and submissiveness. What makes Paula advance also makes her retreat. She is heading for marriage but she is lukewarm about committing herself too early even when she is strongly attracted.

The clash between the sense of the past and the sense of the present is a theme developed and sustained in the novel. The principal characters are Somerset, an architect, and Paula an heiress. Somerset is very much interested in Gothic architecture while Paula admires everything that is modern. The conflict continues as Paula refuses to accept the ceremony of baptism by total immersion. While representing a modern type of woman vacillating between conformity and unconventionality, she resembles Sue Bridehead in *Jude the Obscure*. Paula and Somerset are uncompromising in their cultural preferences as well as by the contrast between her inherited wealth and his desire to pursue a profession. The novel reflects some of Hardy's own longstanding preoccupations in Somerset's quest for a career and his concern for the ethics of architectural restoration.

The tireless plots of the villain, Dare, make the course of love between Somerset and Paula a stormy one as the lovers are kept apart by a series of misunderstandings engineered by Dare. Finally, after the couple is at last united, the castle inherited by Paula is burnt down by Dare and they resolve to leave it as a ruin and build a new house beside it. Both are now prepared to accept the modern spirit in its architectural embodiment.

For the intellectual background of *Two on a Tower*, Hardy made a departure from architecture to astronomy. His aim in this novel was to set the emotional history of two infinitely small lives against the stupendous background of the stellar universe and he undertook some technical research for the purpose.

The hero, Swithin St. Cleeve, is a handsome youth who has a passion for astronomy. He is the son born out of a socially unfortunate marriage between a curate and a farmer's daughter. He has received good education and lives in his grandmother's humble cottage.

Lady Constantine is the lady of the manor and lives in the Great House. She is unhappily married to a man who ill-used her and set off to hunt lions in Africa leaving her behind. Living in the heart of country, she is completely detached from the rural society and is indifferent to its occupants. She meets Swithin in an old tower where he pursues his astronomical observations. Much of the action of the novel as well as the ending of the story take place there.

Lady Constantine is haunted by time as she is some ten years older than Swithin and this barrier ultimately proves more potent than their social inequality in destroying the possibility of happiness. The vacuum in Lady Constantine's life is soon filled first by Swithin and then by her love for him. He is slow in reciprocating her feelings, for his passion at first is exclusively intellectual.

The death of Lady Constantine's husband leaves her comparatively poor and thus levels the distinction between them. Hence, Lady Constantine and Swithin plan to marry in secret.

News, then, reaches Lady Constantine that her first husband is indeed dead but his death was originally reported as having taken place earlier than was in fact the case. She, therefore couldn't be legally married to Swithin.

She then resolves not to marry Swithin and encourages him to travel in pursuit of his astronomical researches until their marriage can take place without the loss of annuity which Swithin inherited from his uncle. In case he marries young, he would forfeit the annuity. Soon after Swithin's departure, Lady Constantine realizes that she is pregnant and, in order to save her name as well as that of her unborn child, is forced to marry the Bishop of Melchester.

After a few years, the bishop dies and Swithin returns with the intention of marrying her but he finds her aged, while he is in his prime. He leaves her but rushes back to announce that he would marry her after all. She dies of shock in his arms and thus the novel concludes with the words that the "bishop was avenged."

The action in the second half of the novel is a muddle of surprises, reverses and improbabilities. There is also an attempt to show the inner conflicts and perplexities of Lady Constantine on whom attention is concentrated.

In *The Mayor of Casterbridge*, Hardy projects the nineteenth century portrait of a man's inner life, rebellion, suffering, loneliness, jealousy and despair. The novel begins with a scene that dominates the analysis of female subjugation. The auction of Susan and his daughter by Michael Henchard at a country fair is clearly an extraordinary event which violates the moral sense of Casterbridge community when it is discovered twenty years later. But there is a sense in which Hardy recognizes the psychological temptation of such a sale, the male longing to exercise his rights over women and to free himself from their burden with a virile decision. This element in the novel could have been articulated by Hardy's Victorian readers but it has been expressed in this context by Irving Howe, "To shake loose from one's wife, to discard that drooping rag of a woman, with her mute complaints and madding passivity, to escape not by a slinking abandonment but through a public sale of her body to a stranger, as horses are sold at a fair. It is with this stroke, so insidiously attractive to male fantasy, that *The Mayor of Casterbridge* begins." (1968: 84)

Howe brings enthusiasm and authority to his exposition of Henchard's motives and he quietly transforms the novel into a male-document. In this exclusive concentration on the sale of the wife, Howe, like most of Hardy's critics, overlooks the simultaneous event, the sale of the child.

Paternity is the central subject of the novel and the ignoring of the sale of the child by critics, perhaps, is becausc the child is a female. For Henchard to sell his son would be so drastic a violation of patriarchal culture that it would wrench the entire novel out of shape. But the sale of a daughter seems almost normal.

Selling his wife and daughter helps Henchard to effectively sever all his bonds with the community of women. Henchard, thereafter, commits his life entirely to the male community, defining his human relationships by the male code of money, paternity and honour. By this act, Henchard also sells out his own need for passion, tenderness and loyalty. The return of his wife, Susan and Elizabeth-Jane, forces Henchard gradually to confront the tragic inadequacy of his codes and the arid limits of patriarchal power. Henchard selling his wife and daughter for five guineas proves the point that man never looked at woman as someone equal and worthy. Lucetta is crushed out of existence by the weight of society's disapproval of her unconventional mode of life.

The Woodlanders exploits a particular Wessex landscape—the woodlands and orchards of North Dorset. It incorporates good examples of the folk customs and traditional practices that Hardy loved to introduce in his novels. Technically, it achieves a much firmer integration of the rustic characters in the main course of the action and it serves in a satisfactorily unobtrusive way, as a context where Hardy was able to explore two topics which greatly preoccupied him in the relationship between the sexes within and outside wedlock.

Grace Melbury becomes a victim of her husband Dr.

Fitzpiers's affairs with Suke Damson and Mrs. Charmond. Since there were no divorce laws at the time, Grace resigned herself to live with her husband in total defeat. The laws were man-made, without any provision for rights of women. She is also partly to be blamed because she betrayed her basic instincts by discarding her lover Giles Winterborne and marrying Dr. Fitzpiers. Marty South is a person with great human capabilities but her aspirations are never fulfilled because of her passivity and probably due to her upbringing to accept her role of a receiver and not a taker. Hardy argues that if women are brought up the same way as men are, they will prove successful. Marty's own words to Grace after Giles's death show that: "In all our outdoor days and years together, ma'am, the one thing he never spoke of to me was love, nor I to him." (400)

Lack of expression is evident in Victorian women and this was condemned by Hardy in his novels.

There is an ambivalence on the class issue with Mr. Melbury and with Grace. Melbury wants to guarantee public respect for his daughter's accomplishments. His admiration for the upper classes and their superior refinement leads him to sacrifice his daughter but at the same time, he is uneasy about dishonouring the understanding with Giles. The effect of the family name of Fitzpiers on George Melbury is predictable: "The touching faith in members of long established families as such, irrespective of their personal condition or character, which is still found among old fashioned people in the rural districts, reached its full perfection in Melbury." (190)

The arrival of the young doctor of gentle birth, Dr. Fitzpiers, tipped the scale against Giles. Fitzpiers's desire to possess Grace overwhelms any consideration and he enters into marriage with the intention of setting up permanently at a sufficient distance from Hintock village. Fitzpiers makes it clear to Grace what actually separates the gentry from the toiling masses. On their way back from honeymoon, he says to Grace: "I do honestly confess to you that I feel as if I belonged to a different species from the people who are working in that yard." (214)

Dr. Fitzpiers is capable of loving more than one woman at once and is already involved with a carnal village-girl, Suke Damson and the wealthy and mysterious widow, Felic Charmond. At the age of thirty, Mrs. Charmond is a restless and dangerously impulsive woman. Hardy describes her as "a creature of strange smouldering erratic passions—kept down like a stifled conflagration but bursting out now here, now there." (233-34) By mere imaginative effort, Hardy lifts her to a remarkable height,

> She was a woman of perversities, delighting in piquant contrasts. She liked mystery, in her life, in her love, in her history. To be fair to her, there was nothing in these which she had any great reason to be ashamed of but her past had never been fathomed by the honest minds of Hintock, and she rarely volunteered her experiences. (234)

The rest of the book is about the differences of sexual mores rather than of class, as though these two spheres of human behaviour are not distinctly separable. In his 1895 preface to *The Woodlanders*, Hardy wrote,

> From the point of view of marriage as a distinct covenant or undertaking, decided on by two people fully cognizant of all its possible issues, and competent to carry them through, this assumption is, of course, logical. Yet no thinking person supposes that, on the broader ground of how to afford the greatest happiness to the units of human society during their brief transit through this sorry world. (5)

It is this conventionality of marriage that Hardy now proceeds to test and examine. A new divorce law would have offered Grace, freedom but such hope of legal freedom is dashed and Grace returns in a defeated state to Dr. Fitzpiers while Giles dies in the cold protecting Grace.

In *Tess of the D'Urbervilles*, Tess who works in a dairy

is raped by Alec D'Urbervilles. Most of her miseries arise from her conventional beliefs. In this regard, Hardy says: "The world is only a psychological phenomenon . . . a cloud of moral hobgoblins by which she was terrified without reason. It was they that were out of harmony with the actual world not she." (114)

Tess's marriage to Angel Clare failed due to Angel's lack of understanding of her situation, her needs and also due to her willingness to endure which is another aspect of her weakness. Her killing of Alec may symbolize her rejection of the cruelty of the muscular world. She had been victimized by circumstances which finally proved beyond her endurance. Her character shows moral and spiritual qualities which qualify her to be a tragic heroine as per Hardy's finest conception of tragedy. According to Hardy, the greatest tragedy is that the worthy is encompassed by the inevitable.

Tess readily accepts the blame and guilt of her reckless parents. For their sake, she accepts employment of the slopes under Alec and surrenders to his evil desires. Her intentions are good. She is pure of heart and is ready to sacrifice her own wishes and interests for the sake of others and willingly endures the unbearable which, in Hardy's view, is her weakness.

Clare knew that she loved him but did not know the full depth of her devotion to him. In his argument to discard the marriage plan, Angel's concern for his own reputation and the fate of their children when the past became known were too much for Tess to bear. Another woman in such a situation might have acted differently.

Tess, like many girls of her time, was seduced by her employer's son and gave birth to a child who eventually died. Angel Clare deserts her after learning of her misfortunes. In order to protect her family from poverty after her father's death, she goes back to her seducer Alec, and murders him when Clare returns unexpectedly to seek a reconciliation. She is arrested and hanged.

Joan Durbeyfield, Tess's mother, is one of the finest of Hardy's secondary characters, superstitious, sentimental, incompetent and impulsive. Nevertheless, she has a prudent eye for the best opportunity. Her secretive and devious nature is the perfect foil to the innocent nobility of Tess. Hardy compares mother and daughter: "When they were together, the Jacobean and the Victorian ages were juxtaposed." (45)

Repeatedly, Tess tries to confide in Angel about her previous rape, only to be thwarted by accident or indecision. As a result, Tess and Angel marry with the fatal words still unsaid till the mutual confession takes place on the wedding-night. Comparing Tess's sin with Angel's admission of being in the company of a stranger for forty-eight hours, does not prevent the display of a double-standard morality. The sympathy that Hardy had evoked for Tess had an impact on Victorian opinion, is easy to understand.

The wedding-night scene is more than an argument, about the social fabric of the nineteenth century, or even more widely about Christian morality in general. Both Tess and Angel find themselves in a crisis of identity as they strive to reconcile the real with the ideal. To Tess's anguished cry, "I thought, Angel, that you loved me—me, my very self," Angel's response is "the woman I have been loving is not you." (264-65)

The woman, Angel claimed he had been loving, was not Tess. She was a figment of his imagination, a private fantasy and no woman at all. In the ideal world, her fate should have been sealed irrevocably as Angel's wife but when he abandons her, she is increasingly made to feel that her true identity lies outside their marriage. The ultimate tragedy of Tess is that of being torn between the ideal and the real. Finally, Tess is about to be arrested, tried and hanged for the murder of her seducer, Alec. She comes to Stonehenge in a mood of total serenity. Her spirit almost dissolves into the great flow of life. Like Henchard, she suffers defeat in a grand fashion. The Mayor of Casterbridge is the epitome of all that is male, a modern Macbeth, going down savagely and bitterly under repeated blows, whereas Tess is the absolute contrast, the totally feminine victim, caught in a web of tragedy by her meekness, generosity and kindness. In the end, she simply surrenders and finds peace and in the famous and provocative comments of Hardy, the novel concludes, "The president of the immortals, in Aeschylean phrase, had ended his sport with Tess." (446)

In the preface to *Jude the Obscure*, Hardy had made it clear that the book was addressed to the men and women of full age and would attempt "to tell without mincing of words, of a deadly war waged between flesh and spirit." (6) Hardy who used the marriage laws in great part as the machinery of the story says: "My opinion at that time, if I remember rightly, was what it is now, that a marriage should be dissolvable as soon as it becomes a cruelty to either of the parties." (8)

Jude the Obscure is more like a game of changing partnerships. What is significant is that the two lesser characters Arabella and Phillotson represent the more conventional, tolerant and conformist elements in the society while Jude and Sue are correspondingly unconventional, rebellious and critical of the social order. Just as Hardy chose to present Tess as a pure woman, so did Hardy in Sue. In effect, Hardy is renewing the questions he asked about the relationship of Tess with Angel Clare and Alec D'Urbervilles: What really does constitute a marriage?

There are four major characters in the story—Jude Fawley, Richard Phillotson, Arabella and Sue, Jude's cousin. Phillotson inspires Jude with a vision of Christminster. Jude learns Greek and Latin, becomes a stone mason in the hope that it would always offer him a job. When it seems his dreams would prosper, he encounters, "The strongest passion known to humanity." (6)

It is embodied in Arabella Donn—a buxom, lusty rather coarse and worldly-wise daughter of a pig farmer. Arabella is Hardy's symbol of the flesh. He stresses her animalism—big breasted fecundity and her blind assertion of the life force pursuing its logical goal. By a pretence of pregnancy, Arabella entraps Jude into marriage. Her confidence is well-founded in the knowledge that hers is the way of the world. Arabella emigrates to Australia and later proposes a divorce which annuls their marriage.

With Arabella gone, Jude makes a fresh attempt to realize

his dream of a scholar's life at Christminster. For the second time, he is distracted by a woman but this time it is a nature very opposite to Arabella's that captivates him. His cousin, Sue Bridehead, is intellectually unorthodox, contemptuous of conventions and stylishly brilliant in a way that dazzles Jude. On one occasion when Jude suggests that they should sit in the Cathedral at Melchester, she says: "I'd rather sit in the railway station . . . that's the centre of the town life now. The Cathedral has had its day!" (160)

Hardy has presented Sue as an unusual and complex character. He has, moreover, carried on, into forbidden areas of speculation where Victorian fiction-reading public was concerned. Jude and Sue, at this stage, are married to different partners but they are soon liberated by divorce. Arabella wishes to legalise her bigamous union with Mr. Cartlett. Phillotson, in his sympathetic and unselfish way, decides to make it possible for Sue now to marry Jude.

However, there is no escape from the tragic forces that are gathering round Jude and Sue. Little Father Time kills the two younger children and destroys himself. She miscarries in consequence and her baby is still-born and the time has come for them to part.

She recollects the solemnity of their original marriages and entertains the thought that she is still Phillotson's wife. Their roles are now reversed. Jude turns to be the agnostic and Sue, the churchworshipper. She returns to Phillotson in a mood of self-mortification and finally Arabella comes back to Jude for the second time but he dies trying to regain Sue. The death of Jude draws a line of finality beneath the complete extinction of all they had stood for.

The Well Beloved is the shortest of Hardy's novels. Hardy points out in his preface in 1912 that it differs from all, the interest aimed at is of an ideal or subjective nature.

Pierston's background is socially ambiguous. His father's commercial success enabled Pierston to train and achieve a growing reputation as a sculptor, creating delicate works of art out of the stone with which his father dealt only in the rough-hewn state.

The Well Beloved is not only a romantic fantasy or a modern fairy-tale but also a fable based on the artist's nature and condition. The most memorable events in this novel are those related to the central preoccupations with the passing of time and the relationship of the past to the present.

Pierston grows older in body but his emotions remain as intense as ever. His attraction to Avice the second leads him to reflect that in his heart he was not a day older than when he had wooed the mother at the daughter's present age. His record moved on with the years but his sentiments stood still. When he is near her, he feels as he had felt when standing beside her predecessor.

The persistence of youthful emotions in undiminished vigour is the source of his creativity as an artist but for the man, it is a penalty which makes him envy the others. The real subject of this novel is not love, but time and age.

Pierston's ambition is to defy time and he meets Avice the third at the very spot where, two generations earlier, he had arranged to meet her grandmother. But even though a renewed copy of his sweet-heart had risen to fill her place, the inescapable truth is, that he himself wasn't renewed.

At the end of the novel, Pierston is compelled to renounce his wish to marry Avice the third. Instead, he marries the shrivelled Marcia who can offer him friendship but not love. With his acceptance of his physical decay, there comes to him placidity, he had never known before. As Pierston accepts the role of an old man for the first time, his emotional life comes to an end. He abandons his studio and finds pleasure in the paintings in the National Gallery than in the crude work of the permanent artist outside. He expresses satisfaction that he has at last gone old and the curse is removed.

Chapter Two

A Feminist Perspective

Feminism is concerned with the emancipation of women by liberating them from man's domination. It demands that women should be treated as autonomous subjects and not as passive objects. What peculiarly signalizes the situation of woman is that she finds herself living in a world where men compel her to assume the status of 'the Other.' Society, being codified by man, decrees that woman is inferior to man. She can do away with this inferior status only by rejecting the male superiority. She, therefore, endeavours to escape from man and no longer seeks to drag him into the realms of immanence—but tries to emerge in the light of transcendence.

To contemporary women, sexual harassment can clearly be seen as a phenomenon arising out of a society which condones male dominance and female subordination. Sexual harassment has been practised on women whenever they have assumed a position to change the authority of the male. In literature, women writers had to contend with the imposition of limitations to their education and their chances to publish and circulate their work. Women's education was intended to provide them with the skills that would make them better wives and mothers. They were to be educated according to the male notion of the ideal woman—one who would support man in his public role while herself remain silent and confined to the private world. Women writers who have ventured into the public realm have all been subjected to male disapproval. The list of women who received negative treatment at the hands of the male literary establishment include Margery Kempe in the fourteenth century, Jane Agnes in the sixteenth century, Aphra Behn in the seventeenth century, Mary Wollstonecraft in the eighteenth century, Harriet Martineau and Emily Dickinson in the nineteenth century and in our own time, Kate Millett who wrote *Sexual Politics* (1970).

Feminists argue that woman should be left alone to live on her own strength and means to fight against the unjust system and obtain her own subsistence and thereby remove her dependant status. According to Simone De Beauvoir, a world where men and women would be equal is easy to visualize. Women reared and trained exactly like men were to work under the same conditions and on the same wages. Sexual act was not to be considered as a service to be paid for. Woman was obliged to provide herself with other ways of earning a living. Marriage was intended to be based on a free agreement which the contracting partners could break at will. Maternity was to be voluntary which meant contraception and abortion were to be authorized.

It is also the contention of the .eminists that a change in women's economic condition alone is not enough to transform her. Though this has been and still remains the basic factor in her evolution, the new woman cannot emerge until the moral, social, cultural and other changes are brought about. Liberty for woman is still an abstract and empty proposition. She can exercise it only in revolt, the only door open to those who have no opportunity to do anything constructive. They must break away from the limitations of their situation and work for their own liberation. This liberation must also be a collective effort and requires, first of all, to build a secure economic condition.

Oppression of women happens to be the main theme of Hardy's major novels which is extensively discussed by feminist theorists as well, who try to find ways to eradicate it. If Hardy's feminism is to be understood in the right perspective, it must be seen in relation to the contemporary feminist theories. Though there was no particular feminist theory as such, yet there are various perspectives. Each one attempts to analyze the topic of women's oppression, its causes and consequences and prescribes strategies for their liberation. However, the feminist theorists have only been able to identify their approach as liberal, Marxist, radical, psychoanalytic, socialist, existentialist and post-modern. Each one of these is only a partial answer to the woman's question. What is fascinating is how these provisional answers join together to explore the ways in which women have been oppressed and celebrate the ways in which many women have managed to take charge of their own destinies.

For liberal feminists, woman's subordination is rooted in a set of conventions and legal constraints that hinder woman's progress. The true potential of woman goes unrealized as she is condemned as being incapable, physically as well as intellectually, by the society. Liberal feminists argue that if woman is given the same civil and educational rights as man, she is bound to achieve eminence in all fields.

Wollstonecraft's *The Vindication of the Rights of Woman* (1792) is basically a plea for equality with men. She argues that women should be educated and allowed to develop their moral and intellectual capacities. In this book, she attacks the concept of femininity and its superficiality. However, feminist writing all through the eighteenth century, concentrated on the issue of 'education' and 'femininity,' and Wollstonecraft, too, has maintained that tradition. Though "education" was her major preoccupation, she has admitted its limitations. She called for a reorganization of society which would be congenial to the development of women.

In the nineteenth century, J.S. Mill differed from Wollstonecraft in insisting that society must provide women not only with the same education, but also with the same civil liberties and economic opportunities that men enjoyed. But like Wollstonecraft, Mill too denied that there were intellectual or moral differences between men and women. Mill argued that any intellectual disparity existing between men and women could be explained as brought about by man's privileged status. It should be noted that Mill was a reformist, not a revolutionary. His book, *On the Subjection of Women* (1869), which was a great feminist statement influenced Hardy's feminist views which he expressed in his major novels. Hardy has dealt extensively in the context of conventionality in marriage, maltreatment of women by men, the unequal divorce laws and the inadequate facilities for women's education. Hence, Hardy's views can be considered identical to those of liberal feminists.

According to the Marxist feminists, women's oppression began with the introduction of "Private Property" that erased whatever the human community had hitherto enjoyed. They strongly hold the view that "Capitalism" is the root cause of women's oppression and if women are to be liberated, the capitalist system must be replaced by a socialist system in which the means of production belong to all. Under socialism, no one being dependent on others, women will be economically independent and equal to men. For liberal feminists, the ideas of individuals account for any change in society, whereas Marxist feminists reject the aforesaid view and stress that production alone is only the primary source of change over time. Marx says: "The mode of production of material life conditions the general process of social, political and intellectual life. It is not the consciousness of men that determines their existence, but their social existence that determines their consciousness." (1972: 20-21)

Friedrich Engels believes that man's control over women is rooted in his control over property and the oppression of women will cease only with the destruction of the institution of private property. According to Engels, the practice of monogamy serves as a means for the transfer of a father's private property to his children. Engels comments: "the first form of the family to be based not on natural but on economic conditions." (1972: 128)

In other words, a monogamous family is not the product of love but of economic power. He contends that male-dominance is simply the result of class-division between the propertied man and the unpropertied woman. He also concludes that if women are to be liberated from the oppression of their husbands, they must first become economically independent. However, Marxist feminists do not discuss issues such as sexuality, double standards of morality and prostitution. Even in their discussions on sex-related issues, there is a tendency to compare sex to work. They consider women's oppression as a class-struggle and do not venture to tackle problems related to oppression imposed on women by men. It is unfortunate that even in socialist systems like the ones existing in China and Russia, oppression of women persists.

For radical feminists, the oppression of women is a fundamental form of oppression. They argue that it is the patriarchal system characterised by power and dominance that oppresses women. In *Sexual Politics*, Kate Millett establishes that patriarchy is a system where male-domination and female submission is achieved through ideological means. According to radical feminists, patriarchy cannot be reformed and therefore can only be destroyed. Hence, they advocate that patriarchy should be destroyed from legal, social, political and cultural institutions. Though the radical feminist's writings are various, one of their important themes is 'the effect of female biology' on woman's function in the private and the public sectors.

In *The Dialectic of Sex* (1970), Shulamith Firestone says that the subordination of women is rooted in the biological inequality of the sexes. She considers relations of reproduction, rather than production, as the driving force in history. She concludes that women's liberation requires a biological revolution and not an economic explanation. Her contention is that women must seize and control the means of reproduction in order to eliminate the sexual differences. In her view, reproduction-controlling techniques such as contraception, sterilization and abortion are sufficient to expunge all sexual roles. Thus, women no longer will have to reproduce as long as technology is able to find ways for people to reproduce.

Hence, women need not be confined to homes, with the result that they will have enough time to labour in the public realm. Her point of view is that when there are no longer, distinct reproductive and productive roles for men and women, it will be feasible to overcome all notions that divide the human community into oppressing males and oppressed females. Sexuality is discussed extensively by radical feminists and that is vital to any woman seeking to understand her personal and political position in society.

According to Ann Oakley, the need for mothering owes nothing to women's biological structure but to the way in which women are socially and culturally conditioned to be mothers. In other words, biological motherhood is not a natural need of women but a cultural construction. She believes that if schools, churches and the media don't emphasize the wonders of motherhood, few girls would grow into women and feel the need to be mothers.

In *Of Woman Born* (1979), Adrienne Rich articulates the difference between the experience of mothering and the institution of motherhood. She argues that women should have the right to decide when to mother and when not, without complying with men's wishes. She believes that if women take control of child-bearing and child-rearing, more mothers would be able to experience biological motherhood on their own terms. She rejects Firestone's plea that female biology has limitation and the only way to liberate women from it is through technology. To Rich, the answer is that women should rear their children with feminist ideals. However, radical feminists have proposed several ways to enable women to escape from the sexual domination of men. They urge women to transform the institution of heterosexuality in favour of celibacy and lesbianism as they insist that men rather than society have forced women into the oppressive gender roles.

For some radical feminists, eradication of gender is the best method to eliminate male-control. In her *Sexual Politics*, Kate Millett finds that sex gender system is the real source of women's oppression. She suggests an androgynous future where the ideal human being combines in himself/herself masculine and feminine traits. Such integration of traits must proceed cautiously. She says: "Androgyny is a worthy ideal only if the feminine and masculine qualities integrated in the androgynous person are separately worthy." (1970: 62)

Millett insists that the androgynous person should combine the most positive and feminine traits. Radical feminism has many shortcomings. It pays scant attention to the issues of race and class. It is also not attentive to the concern of women about colour or poverty. We think that radical feminism should be expansive enough to include those women who believe that racism is more oppressive than sexism.

In spite of their limitations, feminists owe much to radical feminism, as the insight that sexuality is the main cause of women's oppression is vital to any woman seeking to perceive her personal and political position in society. Radical feminists have shown how women's bodies can be used by men against women and also how they can be used by women themselves against women. They teach women how to celebrate their nature and how sexuality can become a source of power for each and every woman in the future.

For psychoanalytic feminists, the centrality of sexuality arises out of Freudian theoretical concepts such as 'the Preoedipal Stage' and the 'Oedipus Complex.' They find the root of woman's oppression hidden deep in her own psyche. To free herself from what is holding her back, women must probe into the depths of their psyche in order to evaluate their position as women. Some psychoanalytic feminists suggest that Oedipus Complex is an invention of men's imagination and women should escape it.

In *The Reproduction of Mothering* (1978), Nancy Chodorow suggests that shared parenting and the involvement of men as primary caretakers of children will have a profound effect on women's sense of gender identity and sexual preference. In her opinion, dual participation in the work-force will change the gender-structure of the Oedipus complex. Authority will no longer be the exclusive property of men and dependence will no longer be the only possession of women. However, psychoanalytical explanations of women's oppression do not provide a comprehensive answer to female subordination as political and economic institutions have not been taken into account. Any change for women should begin from within the individual woman herself and this will provide her with a positive attitude to think of herself as a new woman.

Social feminism is largely the result of Marxist feminist dissatisfaction with the gender-binding character of Marxist thought. They reject, the tendency of Marxists to regard women's oppression as less important than workers' oppression. Therefore, many socialists became convinced that living in a class-society is not the only primary cause of women's oppression. They find that socialist as well as capitalist women remain in the grip of patriarchy. To overcome the limits of Marxist, radical and psychoanalytical feminism, socialist feminists have developed two different approaches—the dual system theory and the unified system theory. These approaches aim at providing a complete explanation of women's oppression.

Juliet Mitchell is an example of a dual-system theorist. She couples a non-materialist account of patriarchy with a materialist account of capitalism. She believes that some aspects of women's life in the family are economic while the others are ideological and social. These social and ideological aspects will remain the same even if there is any change in the mode of production. Mitchell believes that any change in the status of women should be accompanied by the defeat of capitalism as well as patriarchy. This can be achieved by changing patriarchy's economic aspects through material means and its social and ideological aspects by nonmaterial means i.e. psycho-analytical means. Juliet Mitchell says: "The Marxist revolutionary must link arms with the Freudian Psychoanalyst in order to effect women's full and final liberation." (1974: 412)

She is convinced that the causes of women's oppression are buried very deep in the human psyche. As she sees it, the attitude towards women will never really change as long as male and female psychology are governed by the phallic symbol. In other words, she suggests that we should use Marxist strategies to topple capitalism and psychoanalytical strategies to overthrow patriarchy.

For unified system theorists, class analysis is not specific. According to Iris Young, division-of-labour analysis is more specific than class-analysis. She argues that class-analysis focuses on the means of production in general terms, while a division-of-labour analysis pays attention to the individual people who do the work in the society. In other words, division of labour analysis can better explain why women get paid less and do the cheap work while men give out the orders and get paid more. However, Iris Young believes that division of labour has the conceptual power to change Marxist-feminist theory which is powerful enough to accommodate the ideas of Marxist, radical and psychoanalytic feminists in a unitary framework.

Simone De Beauvoir's *The Second Sex* (1949) plays an important role in understanding existentialist feminism. It has helped many feminists to understand the full significance of a woman's 'Otherness.' Though radical, psychoanalytic and Marxist feminists have important things to say about the causes of women's oppression, Beauvoir sees that none of them truly demonstrates why woman is always 'the Other.' Beauvoir argues that the emancipated woman should seek professional autonomy and financial independence. She also encourages women to be intellectual and to study writers such as Emily Bronte, Virginia Woolf and Katherine Mansfield who have been able to probe the sufferings of women. She concludes that women will always be restricted by the kind of existence that has been allotted to them. Therefore, women should create a special space for themselves if they want to be free.

Jean Elshtain criticizes Beauvoir's concept that woman's independence is won at the cost of rejecting her reproductive capacities. For her, immanence and transcendence, essence and existence are ideas that do not arise directly out of woman's lived experience. Feminists generally emphasize unity and integration. They attempt to integrate all aspects of a woman's life and produce a unified feminist theory.

For post-modern theorists, such unity is neither feasible nor desirable as women's experiences differ from those of men due to racial and cultural reasons. They argue that the more feminist thought they have, the better. Helene Cixous encourages women to develop a method of writing that is not restricted by the rules that currently control language. For Cixous, feminine-writing is not merely a new style of writing but it is, "The very possibility of change, space that can serve as a springboard for subversive thought, the precursory movement of a transformation of social and cultural standards." (1981: 249) She believes that by developing feminine writing, women will change the way the world thinks about them and their place in it as well. Julia Kristeva differs from Helene Cixous. She rejects Cixous's identification of 'the feminine' with biological women and 'the masculine' with biological men. She thinks that boys can identify with their mothers and girls can identify with their fathers and while boys can write in a feminine mode, girls can write in a masculine mode. In her estimation to insist that women write differently from men because of their biological differences, is to force patriarchy's oppressive rules on men and women.

For some critics, the rejection of post-modern feminism is based on the dismissal of academics as separate from the real world. They criticize post-modern feminists for using language and ideas in such a specific way that no one else can understand them.

However, these feminist perspectives are only attempts to explain women's subordination and oppression. Thus, it is a major challenge to contemporary feminism to reconcile with the pressure to be different from those who demand integration. It is vital to develop co-ordination and a comprehensive understanding among the various groups of feminists. Otherwise, it will be very difficult to lay claim to what is good and what is bad for women. We believe that such coordination can make feminists achieve their goals and help them to eradicate women's sufferings concretely.

Chapter Three

Under the Greenwood Tree

In his correspondence with Macmillan and Co. in 1871, about the publication of *Under the Greenwood Tree* (1872), Thomas Hardy made it clear that he considered the novel as a story of rural life. *Under the Greenwood Tree* was written in response to the criticism of Hardy's earlier novel *Desperate Remedies*. It is more than just a conventional novel. Hardy placed it among his "Novels of Character and Environment" which he considered to be uninfluenced works. It is his smallest work in content as well as in ideas and similar to the *Trumpet-Major*.

In spite of all this, Hardy shows his penetrative skill in handling Fancy Day and her unconventional actions throughout the novel. His criticism of the conventional mores is rather hinted than expressed profoundly due to the pressures of the publishers. This has been mentioned clearly in his preface to the novel in 1912.

The novel concentrates on Fancy Day's choice of her lovers—Dick Dewy, Fred Shiner and Arthur Maybold—and how she makes up her mind about making one of them her life-partner. Her choice is made in relative freedom from most tangible forms of female dependency, parental control and direct financial pressures. But differences in education and class among her various lovers accentuate the gap between them and her, making her choice rather difficult and at times even confusing. Moreover, these factors bring along a series of misgivings too, before the final choice is made as she settles down for a married life with the young and handsome Dick Dewy.

Fancy Day is a qualified school-teacher with excellent academic achievements. Her father is a game-keeper and a well-to-do man in yalbury wood. These factors allow Fancy Day to hold a good social position. Ever since her arrival at Mellstock, she has become the centre of attraction with an upsetting effect upon the hearts of local young men due to her great charm, social standing and her talent at playing the musical organ. Dick Dewy, Fred Shiner and Arthur Maybold vie with one another for her attention. Arthur Maybold, the young vicar of Mellstock Parish, becomes her lover some time later.

Dick Dewy, though a good looking young man with a bright future of becoming the branch manager of his father's flourishing business, is less eligible in Geoffrey Day's opinion as he is a farmer's son. Geoffrey Day considers Shiner, the church warden, his future son-in-law and persuades Fancy to make up her mind and give her approval. Maybold does not come out openly with his romantic intentions until Fancy puts up an admirable performance at the inaugural function. Fancy Day, with help and advice from Elizabeth Endor-field who is thought to be a witch, brings round her father to give in to her choice of Dick Dewy.

Geoffrey Day, who is a snob, sees marriage as a means of establishing higher social status while recommending Shiner as the best suitor for his daughter. Hardy argues that marriage is not to be decided on economic and social considerations but on the basis of love. Geoffrey Day snubs Dick Dewy when he asks him for Fancy's hand.

> "I'll just tell'ee you've come on a very foolish errand. D'ye know what her mother was?"
>
> "No."
>
> "A teacher in a landed family's nursery, who was foolish enough to marry the keeper of the same establishment." (170)

He explained to Mr Dewy the reason behind her education. "That if any gentleman, who sees her to be his equal in polish, should want to marry her, and she want to marry him, he shan't be superior to her in pocket. Now do ye think after this that you be good enough for her?" (171)

Geoffrey Day brags of educating Fancy in order to lift her up to a superior level which cannot be matched by the people of Mellstock Quire. He thinks of his daughter as a piece of human coinage which he can use in order to buy higher social status. He refuses to acknowledge that Fancy has individuality of her own and can decide for herself. He ignores the fact that women are to be educated seriously in order to develop their intellectual and moral capacities. In this regard Juliet Mitchell says: "At the beginning of the nineteenth century, women had virtually no rights at all. They were the chattels of their fathers and husbands. They were bought and sold in marriage." (1976: 381)

Fancy Day shares her father's susceptibility to external factors and influence in addition to good breeding. Throughout their courtship, Dick is made painfully aware that she cared less for him than for herself and that she was superior to him. Dick was indignant at Fancy's admiration of superficial manners. He thought of her as "A girl, whose feelings though warm, were not deep; a girl who cared a great deal too much how she appeared in the eyes of other men. What she loves best in the world, he thought, with an incipient spice of his father's grimness, is her hair and complexion. What she loves next best, her gowns and hats what she loves next best, myself, perhaps!" (55-56)

Mary Wollstonecraft shares Hardy's protest against woman's vanity and false refinement and sees it as an obstacle against woman's progress and liberation: "In short, women, in general . . . have acquired all the follies and vices of civilization, and missed the useful fruit . . . their senses are inflamed and their understandings neglected, consequently they become the prey of their senses, delicately termed sensibility, and are blown about by every momentary gust of feeling. Civilized women are therefore so weakened by false refinement, that, respecting morals, their condition is much below." (1995: 68-69)

In contrast to Dick's warm and undivided love for Fancy, her emotions are not deep and she lets herself be attracted by one man and another in proportion to how much they feed her vanity. When Dick compliments Fancy on seeing her all dressed up, she remarks: "I like to hear you praise me in that way, Dick. It is meat and drink to a woman. Do I look nice, really?" (185)

Fancy Day accepts Parson Maybold's offer of marriage without thinking of Dick Dewy's love. She considers Maybold suitable solely because he is placed much above her, socially. Later, Maybold discovers Fancy's engagement to Dick Dewy and asks for an explanation. She writes to him saying: "It is my nature—perhaps all women's—to love refinement of mind and manners; but even more than this, to be ever fascinated with the idea of surroundings more elegant and pleasing than those which have been customary. And you praised me, and praise is life to me. It was alone my sensations at these things which prompted my reply. Ambition and vanity they would be called; perhaps they are so?" (200)

Simone de Beauvoir attributes women's vanity to the limitations of their situation even though she recognizes its devastating effects. In this context, she says in *The Second Sex*: "She considers little things important for lack of any access to great things, and, further more, the futilities that fill her days are often of the most serious practical concern to her. She owes her charm and her opportunities to her dress and her beauty. She often appears to be lazy, indolent; but the occupations available to her are as empty as the pure passage of time." (1988: 615) Simone de Beauvoir expresses the fact that women's horizon is closed and if women are called for concrete action, they are as bold and courageous as men.

One evening, Fancy Day who was in a dull mood felt very weary living alone and wondered how miserable it would be to return to yalbury under the rule of her strange-tempered step-mother; that it was far better to be married to anybody than do that. She was impatient at the thought of having to live through the next eight or nine long months before her marriage could take place. The novel ends somewhat in a compromise. Fancy makes her final choice and gets married to her steady lover Dick Dewy. Hardy is doubtful of the future happiness of the newly married couple for want of mutual trust. Fancy Day should have told Dick about her previous acceptance of Maybold's offer of marriage instead of admitting to a little flirtation with Shiner. Hardy believes that mutual understanding and frankness are essential keys to a successful marriage. This is hinted when Dick says: "We'll have no secrets from each other, darling, will we ever?—no secrets at all." "None from to-day," said Fancy. (222) No sooner these words were uttered by the newly weds than a nightingale from a nearby thicket gave a loud and inviting call that reminded Fancy of a secret from her recent past, which she would never tell.

Hardy highlights a few of Fancy's accomplishments—her education, self-confidence and her ability to decide for herself and draw her destiny especially in her choice of her life-partners. Hardy attributes these merits to her good education and well-to-do family background. What Hardy denounces in Fancy's character is her vanity, her ficklemindedness and her craving for praise. Her emotions get easily swayed by praise. She is not consistent in her romantic attachments to either Dick or Maybold. She accepts Maybold's marriage-offer even when she is engaged to Dick, a fact she doesn't make known to Maybold. In her answer to Maybold's letter, she requests him to keep their previous night's meeting and all that passed between them for ever a secret.

Fancy Day was afraid that such a secret would utterly blight the happiness of Dick Dewy, a trustworthy and generous man whom she still loves and will always love. Maybold advises her: "Tell him everything; it is best. He will forgive you." (200)

Fancy's choice of her various lovers can be understood as an exercise of her will and independence, being brought up in a restricted atmosphere of conventions and habits. Hardy has shown his vehement appreciation for women like Fancy Day who defied the conventional norms of the Victorian age by choosing what is good for her. Fancy is seen making some efforts to impose some changes in the manners and etiquettes in public. At her wedding celebration, she instructs the members of her family not to use words like 'Thou' as they are outdated and also not to draw the back of their hands across their mouth after a drink which was too ancient a habit so very humiliating to persons of newer taste.

Change and modernity are introduced into the lives of the simple people. The beauty of it all lies in the smooth transition—the old ways and practices giving way to the new ones without causing bitterness even against earlier stiff opposition, through gentle persuasion by the tactful young vicar. Once the country folk are made to understand the need for change, they render whole-hearted support and co-operation and all objections die down quietly and all are happy in the end. The young parson Maybold and Fancy Day are solely responsible for this.

Under the Greenwood Tree casts a nostalgic look at the rural society. The social changes can be discerned in Fancy and Parson Maybold. The defeat of the choir is followed by the marriage of Dick and Fancy but the changes begin to take place. In his later major novels, the process of change becomes more evident and Hardy is forced to admit its inevitability. The theme of external nature and sexual love remains within the safe boundaries of this pastoral novel.

In his preface to the novel, Hardy implies the limitations of the pastoral genre in expressing his uncompromising vision of social change and alternation. He says: "In re-reading the narrative after a long interval there occurs the inevitable reflection that the realities out of which it was spun were material for another kind of study of this little group of church-musicians than is found in the chapters here penned so lightly, even so farcically and flippantly at times. But circumstances would have rendered any aim at a deeper, more essential, more transcendent handling unadvisable at the date of writing." (1) Here, Hardy wishes that his treatment had been as serious as the theme demanded. *Under the Greenwood Tree* must be taken seriously as it is the first testimony of Hardy's fiction and his maturity.

Chapter Four

Far from the Madding Crowd

In *Far from the Madding Crowd* (1874) we encounter Bathsheba Everdene, who is the first of Hardy's heroines to face life squarely. She has no parents and that accounts for her independence of action and behaviour. It seems that Hardy is trying to do something more ambitious with her than he had attempted with his earlier heroine, Fancy Day in *Under the Greenwood Tree.*

In *Far from the Madding Crowd,* Bathsheba Everdene inherits her uncle's farm and moves into Weatherbury village to take over its management. Gabriel Oak who is just beginning to establish himself as an independent shepherd-farmer is in love with her. After a financial disaster caused by the death of his sheep, he finds employment on Bathsheba's farm. William Boldwood is also in love with Bathsheba but she refuses to marry either of them. In a chance meeting, Bathsheba is overawed by Sergeant Troy, a dazzling young soldier. At first sight, they fall madly in love with each other. Troy deserts Fanny Robin who is pregnant with his child at this time.

Bathsheba hastily enters into marriage with Troy without knowing anything about Troy's past, especially his affair with Fanny Robin. A few months after their marriage, Troy deserts Bathsheba making it look like a case of accidental drowning. Finding herself in the situation of a widow, Bathsheba, after much hesitation, accepts a proposal from Boldwood and agrees to marry him, not knowing that Troy is still alive. At this juncture, Troy makes a surprise appearance and in an unpleasant encounter with Boldwood, gets killed. Consequently Boldwood is confined to prison.

Far from the Madding Crowd is about adultery, misuse of women by men, marriage and death, a theme which is common in Hardy's major novels. As women are the leading characters in Hardy's novels, we are not surprised to find Bathsheba being given a pivotal role. Desmond Hawkins calls her "the most normal and natural of Hardy's heroines." (1976: 52)

Bathsheba's pride and vanity are her most vulnerable points on which the whole action hinges. When Gabriel Oak sees Bathsheba for the first time, his impression about her was that she is vain about her looks. Bathsheba enters her wagon and proceeds to look at herself in the mirror.

> What possessed her to indulge in such a performance in the sight of the sparrows, blackbirds, and unperceived farmer who were alone its spectators,—whether the smile began as a factitious one, to test her capacity in that art,—nobody knows; it ended certainly in a real smile. She blushed at herself, and seeing her reflection blush, blushed the more. (16)

Here, Hardy depicts the most original of all women's sins, for it was through an appeal to her vanity that Eve was persuaded to eat the apple. Mary Wollstonecraft in her book *A Vindication of the Rights of Women* explains the causes of women's vanity and sees vanity as an obstacle in the path of their liberation and freedom. She remarks: "Women are told from their infancy, and taught by the example of their mothers, that a little knowledge of human weakness, justly termed cunning, softness of temper, outward obedience, and a scrupulous attention to a puerile kind of propriety, will obtain for them the protection of man; and should they be beautiful, everything else is needless, for, at least, twenty years of their lives." (1995: 22) Women should not place much importance on external things but on individuality. They must not consume their life in fulfilling male fantasies.

In another incident, in response to Bathsheba's indifferent behaviour to the gatekeeper, Oak remarks: "She has her faults

. . . and the greatest of them is well, what it is always . . . vanity." (18) This is said by Oak in relation to Bathsheba's carelessness to thank him for making the payment of two-pence, over which the gatekeeper was holding her and her wagon from passing.

Bathsheba's vanity betrays her again when she encounters Sergeant Troy in darkness and her dress is caught in his spur. She allows herself to be drawn into a mesmerising chat with him. Though she wants to snub him, she is unable to resist his compliments. In this connection the novelist says, "Her tone and mein signified beyond mistake that the seed which was to lift the foundation had taken root in the chink. The remainder was a mere question of time and natural changes." (166)

There is no doubt that Bathsheba gets dazzled by Troy's flamboyant sexuality and such incidents played an important role in her hasty marriage to Troy. Simone de Beauvoir says: "A naive young girl is caught by the gleam of virility, and in her eyes male worth is shown, according to circumstances, by physical strength, distinction of manner, wealth, cultivation, intelligence, authority, social status, a military uniform; but what she always wants is for her lover to represent the essence of manhood." (1988: 654)

As a girlish prank, Bathsheba sends an anonymous valentine letter to her neighbour, Farmer Boldwood, without pausing to think of the effect made on this lonely man. Boldwood assumes the Valentine letter to be seriously intended and the intensity of his inner life is suddenly released revealing an unexpected emotional outburst. He becomes Bathsheba's distracted suitor. His calm and even dull-looking personality conceals his turbulent life. Hardy comments,

> That stillness, which struck casual observers more than anything else in his character and habit, and seemed so precisely like the rest of inanition, may have been the perfect balance of enormous antagonistic forces—positives and negatives in fine adjustment. His equilibrium disturbed, he was in extremity at once. (118)

We can see that Boldwood's state of mind moves rapidly from one pole to the other when he receives Bathsheba's provocative Valentine letter. Ironically, Boldwood, the stoic misogynist who never cares about women, becomes a passionate lover. Hardy shows his disapproval of Bathsheba's act of folly in sending Boldwood a valentine card by commenting "So very idly and unreflectingly was the deed done." (98)

Hardy condemns such acts of folly and vanity because he believes that such vices are symptoms of fundamental unreliability of women and will obstruct their road to independence and freedom. As one's behaviour is ruled by emotion rather than reason, the behaviour would be subject to a changeable impulse. In defence of reason, Mary Wollstonecraft says: "In fact, the conduct of an accountable being must be regulated by the operations of its own reasons or on what foundation rests the throne of God?" (1995: 41)

Hardy apparently conceives *Far from the Madding Crowd* as a novel of moral education in which bitter experience would gradually purge his heroine, Bathsheba, of her weakness and initiate her into responsibility. The process of change takes place through Bathsheba's relationships with the other characters in the novel. *Far from the Madding Crowd* develops around Bathsheba's changing relations with the three male characters: the undemanding Oak who works patiently for her, protecting her interests as best as he could, Boldwood to whom she owes an obligation because of her whimsical gesture in sending a valentine card with the words, "Marry Me" when she was not at all serious about it and Troy, who fascinates her with his youthful sexuality and extraordinary abilities in various fields, especially his skill at sword-fighting.

Gabriel Oak is a rising young sheep farmer who is financially ruined when his flock is driven over a rock by a dog. He starts over again by becoming a servant to the woman farmer, Bathsheba, who with remarkable coolness commands and demands. Consequently, Oak's hope of marrying Bathsheba is ruined. Hardy describes Oak as "a man whose moral colour was a kind of pepper and salt mixture." (14) To Bathsheba, Oak is unexciting. Hence, she refuses his proposal of marriage. When Oak accuses her of running after him, she retorts back,

> I hate to be thought men's property in that way, though possibly I shall be had some day. Why, if I'd wanted you I shouldn't have run after you like this; 'twould have been the forwardest thing! But there was no harm in hurrying to correct a piece of false news that had been told you. (37)

This statement reflects that Bathsheba is an independent person who can decide for herself regardless of being right or wrong. To Oak's persistent question as to why she wouldn't marry him, she says that she was better educated than him, and if he wanted to marry at all, he should marry a woman with money and who has a larger farm than what he had then. Bathsheba did not value Oak's confession of his ardent and sincere feelings towards her. Oak showed his devotion by saying that he would do one thing in his life which is to love her and long for her and keep waiting till he dies.

There are other instances in which Bathsheba acts out of vanity and pride. For example, she orders Oak to leave the farm when he speaks to her about her unfair treatment of Boldwood and her new friendship with Sergeant Troy as she did not want anyone to lecture her. Besides being rude, she also adds in an arrogant way that she was in charge of the place.

Hardy condemns Bathsheba's vanity but at the same time he sympathizes with her as she is young and inexperienced in the ways of the world. For example, Hardy shows his pity and mercy for Bathsheba who does not know the other side of Boldwood's disturbed character:

> Had she known Boldwood's moods her blame would have been fearful, and the stain upon her heart ineradicable. Moreover, had she known her present power for good or evil over this man, she would have trembled at her responsibility. (119)

When we look into Bathsheba's relation with Boldwood, there is no trace of any romantic or serious intentions at all from her side. The incident of sending Boldwood a valentine card was only a girlish prank that Bathsheba and her companion Lydia Smallbury together played on him on the eve of St. Valentine Day. Bathsheba did not pause for a moment to think of the effect it was going to have on the lonely man. Boldwood, though forty years of age, was very handsome, rich and well-respected in the village. He was regarded till now as a confirmed bachelor. Before the receipt of Bathsheba's Valentine Card, Boldwood is, as Liddy puts it, "a hopeless man for a woman." (78)

Boldwood's recoil from women and the whole range of emotions and human connections makes him live in a misogynistic situation. His lack of interest in Bathsheba at a time when other local farmers show their admiration proves this point. Boldwood's life has the pious style of the monk as Hardy describes it: "Here, in the quiet of Boldwood's parlour, where everything that was not grave was extraneous, and where the atmosphere was that of a Puritan Sunday lasting all the week." (99) This grave atmosphere clings to him even after he has become Bathsheba's distracted suitor.

However, the valentine message plays havoc on Boldwood's emotions. He is terribly disturbed and spends sleepless nights. The intensity of his desires suddenly gets out of control and results in an unexpected emotional outburst. Boldwood finally finds enough courage to approach Bathsheba directly and says: "My life is not my own since I have beheld you clearly, Miss Everdene—I come to make you an offer of marriage." (124)

Bathsheba suddenly realizes the serious consequences of the valentine letter. She makes it clear to him that though she respects him, she cannot marry him. She shows her regret for her irrational behaviour saying,

> I—I didn't—I know I ought never to have dreamt of sending that Valentine—forgive me, sir—it was a wanton thing which no woman with any self-respect should have

> done. If you will only pardon my thoughtlessness, I promise never to. (125)

In spite of Boldwood pleading with Bathsheba, she cannot accept his offer of marriage. She admits that she is wicked to make him suffer. We see Bathsheba learning from her mistakes due to her wanton vanity which Hardy denounces throughout the novel. Bathsheba, on her part, resolves never to interrupt Boldwood's life again. But the mysterious disappearance of Troy brings Boldwood back to the centrestage of Bathsheba's life hoping to marry her.

Bathsheba's relation with Troy was a sudden encounter in the dark, one night when she was looking round to see if all was well and safe about her horses. Her dress got hooked with Troy's spur and it nearly put her off balance. She is dazzled by Troy's flamboyant sexuality. Hardy describes the scene: "The man to whom she was hooked was brilliant in brass and scarlet. He was a soldier. His sudden appearance was to darkness what the sound of a trumpet is to silence." (156)

Bathsheba gets dazzled by Troy's brass and scarlet. Being an aristocrat and well-educated lady, she considers Troy as an exceptional lover. She allows him to flatter her about her beauty as her pride betrays her in failing to recognize Troy's faults and pretensions.

Bathsheba's sin can be categorized as her abasement before a sexual man, Troy who was merely interested in his conquest. As for Troy, he marries Bathsheba to humiliate her as he is incapable of loving her or any other woman. Troy's love of women is mingled with dislike and fear. Hardy describes his feelings towards women: "He had been known to observe casually that in dealing with womankind the only alternative to flattery was cursing and swearing. There was no third method. 'Treat them fairly, and you are a lost man.'" (162)

Troy's misogynistic attitude towards women resembles that of Boldwood's. In the course of the novel, Troy flatters and curses women a good deal, and he does finally become a lost man. Hardy criticizes Troy's indifferent attitude towards women which must change. For Bathsheba as well as Troy, it was only an infatuation which was mistaken for ardent love, yet neither of them was able to check it. Instead, they allow themselves to be drawn deeper and deeper into aimless relationship which results in a hasty marriage.

However, Troy's affection is directed towards Bathsheba's former servant, Fanny Robin. Troy had intended to marry Fanny but he couldn't because Fanny went to the wrong church. Therefore, she had to pay a savage price for a moment's carelessness. From such incidents, it can be seen that Troy's marriage to Bathsheba was based not on true love and understanding but on infatuation and desire. Hardy does not hesitate to show us that a loveless marriage is a constant source of misery and torture to the contracting partners. Miriam Brody says in this regard: "The relations of husband and wife to each other and of parents to children are relations governed by principles cemented by affection; but the reason these feelings will endure is that they are based in rationality." (1983: 49)

Fanny Robin is so central to the plot of the novel that she might also be regarded as a major character. She is the woman Troy is engaged to, whom he abandons for Bathsheba and who dies in childbirth in Casterbridge workhouse. We see Troy's brutal maltreatment of his women, Bathsheba and Fanny Robin. Having seen Fanny and her child lying dead in the coffin, Bathsheba feels the trace of masculine betrayal which was "the conclusive proof of her husband's conduct." (277) Here, Bathsheba realizes her act of folly in marrying Troy who was interested only in his conquest of her. Bathsheba's feelings are mixed. On the one hand, she wishes that she were dead. On the other hand, she wants to recriminate Fanny as if she were still alive. Bathsheba prays for Fanny and places flowers on her head as she comes to know that she and Fanny are both victims of Troy's maltreatment. In regard to man's infidelity, Miriam Schneir comments: "He has created a false public sentiment by giving to the world a different code of morals for men and women, by which moral delinquencies which exclude women from society, are not only tolerated, but deemed of little account in man." (1996: 79-80)

Bathsheba attacks Troy by saying, "This woman is your victim; and if not less than she." (281) Bathsheba's private agony soars high when Troy kisses Fanny and boldly says that "This woman is more to me, dead as she is, than ever you were, or are, or can be." (281) Troy blames Satan for tempting him with the beautiful face of Bathsheba and hampering him from marrying Fanny. Linda Shires says: "Fanny is the truer wife because she has produced his child, because she is a mother, while Bathsheba is not." (1991: 172)

When Bathsheba wants to know from Troy about her own marital status in the present situation, Troy retorts heartlessly: "You are nothing to me—nothing; . . . A ceremony before a priest doesn't make a marriage. I am not morally yours." (282)

Hardy draws our attention to the fact that just a contract cannot make a marriage and marriages should be based upon mutual trust and understanding between men and women. Miriam Brody asserts: "rather than sexual adventure outside marriage, the ideal demanded fidelity and chastity for men and women." (1983: 46)

Fanny's physical sufferings are in a way balanced with Bathsheba's grief as she learns the whole truth about her husband in whom she had blindly put all her trust. Fanny dies in misery but her death is interpreted as a kind of victory and that is evident in Hardy's naming the chapter where Bathsheba discovers the truth as "Fanny's Revenge." The title shows Hardy's consistent defence of women's rights and aspirations.

Hardy conceives *Far from the Madding Crowd* as a novel of moral education meant to purge Bathsheba of her vanity. The character of Bathsheba Everdene is a logical development of the innocently vain village girl, Fancy Day of *Under the Greenwood Tree*. Hardy attacks the vanities of Fancy Day and Bathsheba in an attempt to educate his heroines that vanity cannot, under any circumstances, lead them to independence but will only destroy their chances of emotional and social security. Bathsheba undergoes a process of purgation from vanity which caused her a lot of sufferings. She comes back to Oak who is a man of virtues and a steady character.

On numerous occasions, Oak acts as Bathsheba's mentor and tolerates her though she ignores him. Yet he continues to love her and strive for her welfare even when she marries another man, Troy. Bathsheba's first impression of Oak is that he is coarse and lacks culture and manner but through time, she learns to value his love and devotion.

Finally, Oak gets married to Bathsheba after the death of her husband, Troy, at the hands of Boldwood. This is the kind of marriage which Hardy recommends as it is based on mutual understanding and love and not on a momentary infatuation. Simone de Beauvoir remarks: "On the day when it will be possible for woman to love not in her weakness but in her strength, not to escape herself but to find herself, not to abase herself but to assert herself—on that day love will become for her, as for man, a source of life and not of mortal danger." (1998: 679)

Finally, we can say that Bathsheba is a fine character, more assertive than Fancy Day. She is tested to the limits of her endurance by the blows of harsh and cruel events that expose her vanity and proclaim her courage to the full. She learns the dire consequences of pride and pretensions as she emerges as an independent woman with a solid judgment. Hardy shows his sympathy and admiration for her character especially in her appearance at Casterbridge Corn Exchange. "In arguing on prices she held to her own firmly, as was natural in a dealer, and reduced theirs persistently, as was inevitable in a woman." (92)

Chapter Five

The Return of the Native

The Return of the Native (1878) is about unfulfilled desires, marital infidelity, unrealized ambitions and the resultant frustration. The heroine of the novel, Eustacia Vye, is in love with Damon Wildeve who later marries Thomasin Yeobright. Thomasin's cousin, Clym Yeobright, returns to Egdon Heath from Paris where he has been working as a diamond trader. In spite of the glamour of Parisian life, Clym decides to stay back at Egdon Heath, work among his people and educate them. Clym's subsequent marriage to Eustacia fails due to lack of mutual understanding. Eustacia wants Clym to go back to Paris and take her out of the suffocating and monotonous life at the Heath but Clym finds living and working among people at Heath as most rewarding and satisfying. However, things suddenly take a turn for the worse when Clym's eyesight fails and he is forced to work as a furzecutter. Under these hopeless and depressing conditions, Eustacia renews her romantic friendship with Damon Wildeve who promises to help her to get out of Egdon Heath secretly. During their attempt, Eustacia and Wildeve get drowned and Thomasin enters into a second marriage with Diggory Venn, a dairy farmer who loves her and Clym finds his vocation as an itinerant preacher.

Egdon Heath occupies a prominent place in the novel. There is no place more remarkable in the Victorian novels than Egdon Heath. The first chapter of the novel is entirely devoted to the place. The Heath is described as a great expanse of the wild, having some energy which is felt by all those who dwell in it. The heath-folk meekly adjust to the harsh nature of the place. Thomasin and Clym also seem to accept its severe conditions but Hardy uses the Heath as a place of depressing, suffocating conventions and traditions that surround his nineteen-year-old heroine, Eustacia Vye. Hardy describes the Heath:

> A Saturday afternoon in November was approaching the time of twilight, and the vast tract of unenclosed wild known as Egdon Heath embrowned itself moment by moment. Overhead the hollow stretch of whitish cloud shutting out the sky was as a tent which had the whole heath for its floor. (3)

Hardy gives yet another account of Egdon Heath a little later: "Civilization was its enemy. Ever since the beginning of vegetation its soil had worn the same antique brown dress, the natural and invariable garment of the formation." (86)

In *The Return of the Native*, Eustacia Vye attempts to escape the boredom and lack of fulfilment imposed on her by her lonely life on Egdon Heath by indulging herself in passionate love affairs. She falls in love with Damon Wildeve, the wealthy owner of Quiet Woman Inn. She finds Wildeve interesting but not adequate. Therefore, she is not interested in marrying him. When she learns about Clym Yeobright's prosperous situation in Paris, she is very anxious to marry him even before meeting him. Hardy has deep sympathy for the way Eustacia feels about her frustrated and empty life. It is her cramped life that leads her to turn to the idea of passionate love as a way of gratifying her need for life and more important as a way of fulfilling herself as a person. Simone de Beauvoir observes in her book *The Second Sex*: "Woman is shut up in a kitchen or in a boudoir, and astonishment is expressed that her horizon is limited. Her wings are clipped, and it is found deplorable that she cannot fly. Let but the future be opened to her, and she will no longer be compelled to linger in the present." (1988: 616) Since her sphere is limited, she tries to fulfill her inborn desire of being loved and is ready to accept all the throbs around her.

Hardy lays much emphasis on Eustacia Vye's relation with Edgon Heath. He defines her as an outsider, an alienated woman barred from useful activity. Eustacia belongs to Budmouth, a fashionable seaside resort, where she has social contacts with high-society citizens. It is the death of her parents that put her under the care of her grandfather who chooses to live on Egdon Heath. She hates the change of location but has no choice and is forced to live there deprived of the good life she enjoyed at Budmouth. The above circumstances drive her to find an outlet for her pent-up emotions so that she could lead a more satisfying life.

Eustacia Vye always prays to God to relieve her from the cruel loneliness of the Heath. "O deliver my heart from this fearful gloom and loneliness: Send me great love from somewhere, else I shall die." (67)

Eustacia is depicted as an ambitious passionate young woman. When she meets Wildeve at the pool-side bonfire, it is a triumphant pleasure for her. She is sure that Wildeve did not marry Thomasin earlier because he loves her. Later, she finds reasons to shift her attention to Clym Yeobright and virtually encourages Wildeve to marry Thomasin.

Eustacia Vye's marriage with Clym is doomed from the beginning since it was based only on the prospect of persuading Clym to return to Paris—the centre of the fashionable world—where she could live a glamorous life and leave the disgusting Heath far behind. But, for Clym, life in Paris is contemptible and unattractive since he had to live in an alien culture. His decision now is to work among the people he knew best and to be useful in their progress. In other words, Clym is ready to give up his name and successful business for the benefit of his fellowmen much against Eustacia's wishes. While Eustacia cannot endure the Heath, Clym feels that the Heath is the most exhilarating and soothing thing. He would rather live on Egdon Heath than anywhere else in the world while for Eustacia, it has to be Paris.

Lack of understanding of Eustacia's needs makes Clym fail to see that she has never given up her worldly ambitions, but believes, instead, that she will make a good teacher. Thus, Eustacia's hopes of getting to Paris remain a delusion and her materialistic ambitions clash with Clym's idealistic ones. Shortly after their marriage, Eustacia requests Clym: "take me to Paris, and go on with your old occupation, Clym. I don't mind how humbly we live there at first, if it can only be Paris, and not Edgan Heath." (249)

Clash of interests is evident here. But if Clym's experience is taken into consideration, it is clear that Hardy views this desire for materialism and its fulfilment as a path that leads to self-achievement. Clym has passed through this stage earlier in his life while for Eustacia, it is a dream yet to be fulfilled. Hardy believes that such a stage cannot be cut out of the natural stages of development. Hardy says in this context:

> in passing from the bucolic to the intellectual life the intermediate stages are usually two at least, frequently many more, and one of these stages is almost sure to be worldly advance. We can hardly imagine bucolic placidity quickening to intellectual aims without imagining social aims as the transitional phase. (174)

The same thing applies to Eustacia who cannot proceed from a stage of ignorance or placidity to intellectuality without going through one of the intermediate stages namely worldly ambition. Hence there is a great desire in Eustacia to go to Paris. Simone de Beauvoir remarks: "Let the future be opened to her and she will no longer cling desperately to the past. When women are called upon for concrete action, when they recognize their interest in the designated goals, they are as bold and courageous as men." (1988: 614)

Hardy's Eustacia Vye is a girl with some forwardness of mind. She possesses an unconventional and rebellious nature. It is unbearable for her to see the Heath. To avoid this sight, she would stay indoors, overhauling the cupboards or humming some ballads. She would sing a psalm on Saturday nights and read the Bible on weekdays to pass her time. Such acts were due to the effect of her unpleasant situation which places her in a strange state of isolation. Mary Wollstonecraft explains woman's restricted situation by remarking: "Confined then in cages like the feathered race, they have nothing to do but to plume themselves, and stalk with mock majesty from perch to perch. It is true they are provided with food and raiment, for which they neither toil nor spin, but health, liberty and virtue, are given in exchange." (1995: 63)

Besides the lack of understanding between Clym and Eustacia Vye, there were other factors that caused unhappiness in their relationship. Such factors are represented in Clym's possessive mother, Mrs. Yeobright and Wildeve, disenchanted with his own marriage to the mild and conventional Thomasin Yeobright. Mrs. Yeobright is very possessive of her son, Clym. She rebukes Clym when she learns that he has left the Paris diamond establishment and compares him with his own father who failed to live up to her expectations: "I suppose you will be like your father: like him, you are getting weary of doing well." (178) Mary Ellen Jordan comments on Mrs Yeobright's attitude: "By failing to acknowledge her husband as a worthy model and by pinning hopes on her son as the 'one idea' which has occupied her since the death of her husband, Mrs. Yeobright compounds the oedipal dilemma of her son and makes it difficult for him to separate from her and strike out his own." (1982: 103).

It is interesting to note that Jemima Hardy, Thomas Hardy's mother, resembles Mrs. Yeobright in some respects, Mrs. Yeobright is intolerant of both Thomasin's and Clym's romantic attitudes. She refuses to back their decisions to marry and strike out on their own and she is unwilling to attend either of their weddings. Similarly, Jemima Hardy did not attend Thomas Hardy's wedding with Emma Gifford. The depiction of Mrs. Yeobright suggests a woman lacking insight into the needs of her children. However, the breach between mother and son does not occur over the issue of Clym becoming a school master though a great tension between them is already established. It is the presence of Eustacia Vye as a potential rival which upsets Mrs. Yeobright. In her opinion,

Eustacia is not the right woman for Clym as she will cause him only sorrow. She calls her a hussy and a dissatisfied woman.

Mrs. Yeobright is utterly shocked at Clym's final decision taken without consulting her. Mrs. Yeobright remarks: "It is incredible to me that a man accustomed to the attractive women of Paris and elsewhere should be so easily worked upon by a girl in a heath." (189) She also asserts that Eustacia is of no use either to herself or to other people. Finally, Mrs. Yeobright forces the breach between Clym and herself: "You have come only to distress me, a lonely woman, and shorten my days! I wish that you would bestow your presence only where you bestow your love." (205)

The strong mother-son relationship is broken and Mrs. Yeobright's death on the Heath without a reconciliation with her own son, Clym, causes an immense grief to Clym which affects him very deeply. In his major novels, Hardy extensively discusses parental relationship and its influence extensively.

The fatal entanglement of Damon Wildeve's marriage with Thomasin Yeobright and Eustacia Vye's with Clym Yeobright bring a dramatic twist to the story. Damon Wildeve, an engineer, abandons his profession and becomes the landlord of a local inn. He is a rich and resourceful man who inherits a fortune after the death of his uncle. Hardy defines his character: "To be yearning for the difficult, to be weary of what offered; to care for the remote, to dislike the near; it was Wildeve's nature always." (216)

There is a resemblance between Damon Wildeve and Frank Troy of *Far from the Madding Crowd*, in their infidelity to their wives. The only thing that can rouse Wildeve to an emotional fever is to see his wife, Thomasin, desired by someone else and that explains his mentality that women are sexual objects to be exploited and possessed. Wildeve is solely responsible for the unfortunate death of Mrs. Yeobright and the misfortune of Eustacia Vye which ends in his as well as Eustacia's tragic death. J.S Mill observes on men's attitude towards woman: "Men do not want solely the obedience of women, they want their sentiments. All men, except the most brutish, desire to have, in the woman most nearly connected with them, not a forced slave but a willing one, not slave merely, but a favourite." (1995: 18)

Hardy analyses Wildeve's nature as erratic and fitful. Being incapable of loving Eustacia Vye, he remains a constant danger in her course of life. When he finds Eustacia Vye feeling miserable, he assures her that he is ready to help her in case she wants to leave the place altogether. At Eustacia's request, Wildeve agrees to help her to reach Budmouth harbour without her grandfather's or husband's knowledge. But, the unsuccessful plan to escape turns out to be the most ill-conceived and fatal one.

In contrast to Wildeve, Diggory Venn has all the virtues of loyalty, resourcefulness and devotion to Thomasin Yeobright, who does not love him until experience has taught her to value him better. Venn's devotion and selfless love for Thomasin surprises Eustacia Vye. "What a strange sort of love, to be entirely free from that quality of selfishness which is frequently the chief constituent of the passion, and sometimes its only one." (152)

Diggory Venn remains devoted to Thomasin for years. Through bad times, he stands beside his beloved, Thomasin. Even when Thomasin refuses his offer of marriage, he continues to strive for her happiness. His intention has been to be close to Thomasin whom he still loves. Such constant love ignites the spark of love in Thomasin's heart. They are finally, duly rewarded with the promise of a contented life together. Diggory Venn resembles Gabriel Oak in his selfless love for Bathsheba Everdene in *Far from the Madding Crowd.*

In *The Return of the Native*, the impression of Eustacia Vye as a tragic heroine with a sense of loss grows out of Hardy's sensitivity to the frustration and helplessness present in Eustacia Vye. Eustacia is undoubtedly a woman of considerable intelligence and ability but ambitious women become self-destructive in a society which has no appreciation for such women. At one place, Wildeve remarks that Eustacia is 'such a rare plant' in such a rare place! Hardy fully sympathizes with her spirit of revolt even though it is misdirected towards materialistic goals. In regard to the conventions of society, Simone de Beauvoir says: "The adolescent girl often thinks that she can simply scorn convention; but even there she is engaged in public agitation; she is creating a new situation entailing consequences she must assume. When one fails to adhere to an accepted code, one becomes an insurgent." (1988: 692)

Eustacia Vye is miserable as she is reduced to living in a cottage with Clym, now a blind furzecutter, who does not understand her needs. It is in such a humiliating and extremely insufferable situation that she plans her escape with a lover for whom she has no respect and whom she considers unworthy of her. However, Hardy views her desperate action, dissipated energies and her triviality with remarkable compassion.

Eustacia Vye and Thomasin Yeobright are two characters with contrasting natures. We see Eustacia as one who is unable to conform to conventions while Thomasin is quite conventional and content in her role as a wife and mother, a typical Victorian woman who accepts the superiority of man over woman and the social norms of the period. Therefore, she is under no psychological pressure to revolt against anything, and revolt is repugnant to her. Simone de Beauvoir explains a woman's passivity: "In a generous woman resignation takes the form of forbearance: she puts up with everything, she condemns no one, because she holds that neither people nor things can be other than they are." (1988: 613)

While Thomasin is carved in the mould of a forbearing woman, Eustacia Vye is a rebel who rejects society's concept of a woman's status. Eustacia's ceaseless search for excitement and love should be interpreted in the context of the boredom and frustration she is made to cope with and not according to Mrs. Yeobright as some sort of innate deficit. Eustacia's depression is traced back to her living in Egdon Heath, a place she never liked. She says to Wildeve: "Tis my cross, my misery and will be my death." (82)

Eustacia Vye's strategy to fight depression is to be passionately in love with attractive men. "To be loved to madness—such was her great desire; love was to her the one cordial which could drive away the eating loneliness of her days." (66) Her need to feel loved is so great that it eclipses her realization of the fact that she is not loved in return. In the case of Wildeve, her pride rebels against her passion for him and she longs to be free but she can be free only under one circumstance and that is, with the arrival of a greater personality than Wildeve. In the case of Clym Yeobright too, Eustacia's love for him is not based upon any proper understanding of his character.

She is attracted to Clym through rumours about his glamorous life in Paris and decides to marry him without seeing him. Her obsession about Clym is based on daydreams and fantasies. With her marriage to Clym, she realizes the difference between her romantic image of Clym and the real Clym who is now her husband. Hence, she goes back to Wildeve, even though she is aware of her foolish act. Her unlawful romantic relationship with Wildeve brings her greater miseries and more disillusions which finally lead to their untimely death.

In the nineteenth century, women were educated so as to be well equipped with the means to find fulfilment in life through family relationships and affections. Such a satisfaction derived from life was regarded to be more than adequate compensation for the restrictions imposed on women by the society. Referring to Rosemarie Tong's book *Feminist Thought*, Mary Wollstonecraft says that women "should be provided with a real education, one that sharpens and focuses her mind and gives her a chance to develop her rational and moral capacities, her full human potential." (1989: 15)

Through his heroine Eustacia Vye, Hardy presents a social situation to show how unsatisfying and how dangerous women's total emotional dependence could be. Hardy's concern can be justified here since dependence is a major hurdle in women's way to progress. We also find that Thomasin's dependence and conventionality are responsible for her sufferings.

Chapter Six

The Mayor of Casterbridge

The Mayor of Casterbridge (1886) highlights the recurring theme in the Victorian novel of the past crime and its inevitable consequences. Hardy examines the Victorian codes of male supremacy through the characterization of Michael Henchard—his inner life, revolt, loneliness and suffering. While attempting to cast off his passionate self, Henchard goes through a process of self-discovery and enlightenment of his own vulnerability. Through the sequence of a number of critical events, we are able to see how Henchard's past crimes catch up with him. Misfortunes befall him in quick succession, beginning with the loss of mayorship. Once again he takes refuge in intoxicating liquors which he abandoned after a religious vow and falls on evil days in the changed circumstances. Finally, in extreme dejection and miserable conditions, Henchard breathes his last as an uncared, unloved and unlamented man, bitterly making himself fully responsible for all his past crimes.

The Mayor of Casterbridge has the most dramatic beginning of Hardy's novels. The highest point of the dramatic action takes place in the opening chapter itself and the rest of the story is woven around the initial error—Henchard's selling of his wife Susan and infant daughter at a public auction in exchange for five guineas. The scene dramatizes the most disgraceful stigma of female subordination and humiliation.

The sale of Susan and her daughter, Elizabeth-Jane, is a sinful act which violates the moral sense of humanity. Such a sale shows Henchard's desire to trade with women as his own property and to free himself from responsibilities whenever he desires. Mill argues: "men should not be trusted with absolute power. Such an absolute power within the family and marriage only leads to brutalization of women." (1995: 42)

Susan's meek acceptance of her fate and the traces of legality with which her poor mind struggles serves to highlight the maltreatment of women in general. There seems to be no law in existence at the time to prevent a woman from being auctioned like cattle at a fair. In his analysis, Hardy places the blame on Susan for her passivity which is the main obstacle of women's progress. In condemning the passive attitude of his heroine, Henchard says:

> Well, I must walk about till I find her . . . seize her, why didn't she know better than bring me into this disgrace! he roared out. She wasn't queer if I was. 'Tis like Susan to show some idiotic simplicity. Meek—that meekness has done me more harm than the bitterest temper! (17)

However, the wife-selling scene is not just an incident created for the sole purpose of intrigue and uniqueness but there had been such practices before. For example a man in a tent at the fair is reported as saying,

> For my part I don't see why men who have got wives and don't want'em shouldn't get rid of 'em as these gipsy fellows do their old horses, said the man in the tent. Why shouldn't they put 'em up and sell'em by auction to men who are in need of such articles? Hey? Why, begad, I'd sell mine if anybody would buy her! (8)

According to Hardy, in the feudal bourgeois society, woman was reduced to a commodity and that was accepted by the society without any qualms. Hardy also points out that a society built on cash nexus cannot but turn human beings into objects and things. Mukherjee and Ramaswamy argue: "The principle that regulates existing marital relations between husband and wife is wrong and unjust. It is a major impediment to the improvement of the human race. On the contrary the principle of equality should be the ordering principle without conceding power or privilege on the one side nor disability on the other." (1995: 1)

Most of Hardy's critics ignore the simultaneous incident which deeply determines Henchard's fate—the sale of the child. Elaine Showalter attributes the critics' attention to the sale of the child, to the fact that the infant was a female. She remarks: "For Henchard to sell his son would be so drastic violation of patriarchal culture that it would wrench the entire novel out of shape; but the sale of a daughter—in this case only 'a tiny girl'—seems almost natural." (1979: 103)

The rejection of the wife who has borne only a female offspring may be attractive to male fantasy. Rosemarie Tong remarks: "To eliminate male control, men and women have to eliminate gender-specificity, sexual status, role, and temperament—as it has been constructed under patriarchy." (1989: 96)

Here, Hardy shows Henchard's reaction after selling his wife and daughter.

> Did I tell my name to anybody last night, or didn't I tell my name? he said to himself; and at last concluded that he did not. His general demeanour was enough to show how he was surprised and nettled that his wife had taken him so literally—as much could be seen in his face, and in the way he nibbled a straw which he pulled from the hedge. (17)

After the sale, Henchard tries to evade the full responsibility of his abominable crime by attributing it to drunkenness and lack of reason and control. Nonetheless, his anger and humiliation can't change the fact that a bargain was struck and the goods were delivered. Henchard's painful realization of his mistake under the influence of strong liquor makes him abstain from drinking for nineteen long years. He also leads a chaste life throughout the long period of separation from his wife. He enjoys the local legend he has created of himself as "the celebrated abstaining worthy." (38)

Henchard's emotional life is not so hard to define as Hardy gives us a few hints of his psyche. He is recognised by his well-known haughty indifference to the society of womankind, his silent avoidance of converse with the sex." (94) Henchard also boasts of himself to Farfrae, as "being by nature something of a woman-hater, I have found it no hardship to keep mostly at a distance from the sex." (81)

Being reduced to the status of an orphan due to the absence of his wife and daughter, Henchard practically severs all his bonds with the society of women. He virtually devotes his life to the male codes of money and business contracts. Owing to this strange behaviour, Henchard deprives himself of the basic human need for passion, tenderness and care in life. Simone de Beauvoir says: "The fact is that today neither men nor women are satisfied with each other. But the question is to know whether this is an original curse that condemns them to rend each other or whether the conflicts in which they are opposed merely mark a transitional moment in human history." (1988: 725) We believe that man's attitude towards women must change and that will lead to their happiness and moral elevation.

Owing to loneliness, Henchard develops an intimate relationship with Donald Farfrae, his employee, to such an extent that he trusts Farfare with all the secrets of his past life. A logical explanation of the strong bond between the two would be a young man's search for a useful employment and a lonely middle-aged man's quest for good company and assistance in conducting his business profitably. However, Henchard seems to have created a rival for himself in the process, for their smooth relationship somehow turns into an unpleasant one. Such a relationship gets further complicated by subsequent business rivalry. Henchard is quite jealous of Farfrae's success and popularity and by dismissing him from service, Henchard disturbs his own peace.

However, Farfrae is almost the opposite of Henchard. Farfrae is a decent and accommodating person with an open disposition. There is a sense of moral and emotional stability in his character. In business, as in love, he will do nothing which is really dishonourable. His honesty, efficiency, business acumen and foresight earn him great respect of the community. Anyway, Farfrae's neglecting of Elizabeth-Jane when he falls in love with Lucetta doesn't tarnish his image. First, he was not aware of Lucetta's involvement with Henchard and secondly, it was due to Henchard's strict warnings that he had to discard Elizabeth-Jane in whom he had shown considerable interest earlier. In fact, his continued concern for Elizabeth-Jane's happiness is a proof of his fairmindedness. Henchard, on the other hand, has a volcanic temper and an impulsive nature. His avoidance of women has an adverse effect on him. When some passion takes hold of him, all his energies are spent towards that passion exposing him to shame which eventually destroys him.

Farfrae serves as a foil to Henchard. He is somehow too ordinary by comparison. Just as he cannot descend to the shameful depths of Henchard, he is incapable of rising to the full stature of Henchard's spiritual grandeur. When we look at Henchard's character, we find that many of his deeds are contemptible. His behaviour towards women remains manipulative. His maltreatment of Susan and his harsh treatment of Elizabeth-Jane when he learns about her true parentage are fine examples. With Lucetta, he uses emotional blackmail to marry her. In order to prevent Farfrae from marrying Lucetta, he plays dirty tricks and stops only on realizing their futility. When Farfrae and Lucetta move into the Mayoral House, Henchard becomes uncontrollably jealous. Henchard's actions can be seen as selfish and manipulative. He prevents Newson from claiming his daughter just because she is the only thing he possessed after the loss of Susan, Farfrae and Lucetta.

Having established Henchard's character in this way, Hardy starts examining the limits of the patriarchal power through some incidents which lead Henchard to discover his own incapacity to love. There are some significant events that have a devastating effect on Henchard. They begin with the estrangement of Farfrae who has been a trusted friend and business advisor. This is followed by the unfortunate demise of Susan whom he has wronged and the revelation of Elizabeth-Jane's real parentage. But the worst of all is the furmity woman's denunciation of Henchard in the court scene. The furmity woman is accused for disrespect for the church but her revelation of Henchard's past crime has been an effective challenge to the authority of the patriarchal law. The furmity woman says in regard to Henchard being a magistrate: "It proves that he's no better than I, and has no right to sit there in judgement upon me." (232) In a derisive manner, she indicts Henchard who is the magistrate sitting in judgement of her crime. Hardy uses the furmity woman to bring out Henchard's disgraceful past into the open. Here, Hardy illustrates how this revelation brings a sudden twist in Henchard's fortunes:

> On that day—almost at that minute he passed the ridge of prosperity and honour, and began to descend rapidly on the other side. It was strange how soon he sank in esteem. Socially he had received a startling fillip downwards; and, having already lost commercial buoyancy from rash transactions, the velocity of his descent in both aspects became accelerated every hour. (251)

Hardy wants to prove how such a crime as Henchard's will never go unpunished. He also makes sure that retribution for Henchard's inhuman act committed in public, should come as a public dishonouring. Hence, Henchard reacts publicly with his withdrawal as a magistrate. This conforms to Hardy's vehement defence of women's rights.

When Lucetta rejects Henchard's marriage proposal and decides to marry Farfrae due to Henchard's disgraceful past, he blackmails her by threatening to reveal to Farfrae her involvement with him. In an attempt to dissuade him, Lucetta arranges a secret meeting with Henchard at the Roman Amphitheatre. She dresses in an unattractive manner in order to discourage Henchard from desiring her. Hardy remarks,

> The unusual plainness of her dress, her attitude of hope and appeal, so strongly revived in his soul the memory

> of another ill-used woman who had stood there and thus in bygone days, and had now passed away into her rest, that he was unmanned, and his heart smote him for having attempted reprisals on one of a sex so weak. (288)

Lucetta's pathetic appearance is deliberately calculated to win Henchard's pity and calm his competitiveness. Although he is wrecked and defeated by a woman, Henchard's understanding of women is still constituted by patriarchal laws. In Hardy's view, there is nothing more devastating than defeat in love for a man of pride and strong will like Henchard.

As the novel progresses, we see Henchard's total decline. His utter disappointments make him turn to liquor. He dreads to think of a future without anyone's company e.g. Susan, Farfrae, Lucetta and Elizabeth-Jane. In this desperate situation, Henchard contemplates suicide but changes his mind on discovering the effigy of himself floating in the stream after the performance of the skimitty ride. Finally, Henchard dies lonely in a small cottage of one of his labourers, Abel Whittle. Elaine Showalter comments: "the effigy which Henchard sees floating in ten Hatches Hole . . . is in fact the symbolic shell of a discarded male self, like a chrysalis. It is the completion of his unmanning—a casting off—of the attitudes, the empty garments, the facades of dominance and authority." (1979: 112)

In regard to the female character of this novel, we find Susan warm-hearted but not shrewd or sharp at all. Susan's unpardonable weakness is her idiotic simplicity and passivity which is not acceptable to Hardy though he admires her endurance. She is simple-minded enough to think that the sale-deed was legal and binding on her. J.S. Mill explains woman's situation: "All women are brought up from the very earliest years in the belief that their ideal of character is the very opposite to that of men; not self-will, and government by self-control, but submission, and yielding to the control of others. All the moralities tell them that it is the duty of woman . . . to live for others; to make complete abnegation of themselves." (1995: 19)

In *The Mayor of Casterbridge*, Elizabeth-Jane is portrayed as a girl of sound character, totally free from vanity and fickleness. She is indeed different from Bathsheba and Eustacia Vye. She is affectionate, though not exactly compassionate. She cannot forgive Henchard for telling her that Newson is not her real father nor when he deliberately prevents Newson from meeting her. We can say that Elizabeth-Jane's intelligence, prudence, fortitude and general stability mark her as one of Hardy's endearing heroines. Probably, nothing in the novel shows so pitifully as Henchard's total incapacity for affection, as his treatment of Elizabeth-Jane after knowing that she is not his daughter. But Elizabeth-Jane has a forgiving nature. Her heart softens towards Henchard in spite of his cruel treatment of her. She also regrets her unkindness towards him at their last meeting on her wedding day. It is Elizabeth-Jane who takes ascendancy while Henchard faces his downfall. In buying and selling, her word was law. Henchard would often consider for hours together the implication of her deeds. It is a humble and yet an educative act through which Hardy seeks to show that more sensitivity and understanding between man and woman is necessary for creating a healthy society. Simone de Beauvoir believes: "When we abolish the slavery of half of humanity, together with the whole system of hypocrisy that it implies, then the 'division' of humanity will reveal its genuine significance and the human couple will find its true form." (1988: 741)

Lucetta is the second woman Henchard has wronged. She is an unconventional woman who leads a free life. She is the only woman who has been romantically involved with Henchard, but he is crushed out of existence by the weight of society's disapproval of her unconventional mode of life. She collapses in a hysterical fit while watching the horrible show of the skimmity ride which is used to publicize her past. Simone de Beauvoir says in this regard: "The woman who does not conform devaluates herself sexually and hence socially, since sexual values are an integral feature of society." (1988: 692)

Looking at the feminist aspect of the novel, we find

Hardy defending his heroines and fighting for their rights. Hardy condemns the male supremacy exercised by Henchard and at the same time he sympathizes with Susan's simplicity and ignorance. He also condemns the docile nature of Susan and her attitude towards her husband. However, we might perceive the story of Henchard as the bending and breaking of the male against the female endurance and tolerance. Showalter remarks: "Stripped of his mayor's chain his master's authority, his father's rights, Henchard is in a sense unmanned." (1979: 103)

Thus Henchard ends as he began, a loner. He has his fatal flaw which leads him into one mistake after another. In any case, neither his suffering nor his bouts of self-accusation help him to survive his stubborn ego. *The Mayor of Casterbridge* was written when the Industrial Revolution was taking place and its effect was felt even in the English countryside. The society showed signs of change with the loss of certain social values such as feudal values, the exploitation of peasants and strong superstitious beliefs. It was a time when education had begun to close the gap between town and country. There was a new attitude towards sex too. Victorian morality had begun to look upon sexual love as something soulful, despite its accompanying agonies. The romance of love did not disappear, but it assumed passionate dimensions in reaching out for fulfilment.

Chapter Seven

The Woodlanders

The Woodlanders (1887) is an account of Little Hintock, the woodland lying in the South of England, its inhabitants, their occupations and their lives on which money, ambition, and intense passion make a powerful impact. It also records how a small village community slowly accepts the changes which modernization introduces in its wake. It is in *The Woodlanders* that Hardy's treatment of the question of marriage becomes more explicit and clear. He tackles the relationship between men and women within and outside the wedlock. In his preface to *The Woodlanders*, Hardy writes:

> From the point of view of marriage as a distinct covenant or undertaking, decided on by two people fully cognizant of all its possible issues, and competent to carry them through, this assumption is, of course, logical. Yet no thinking person supposes that on the broader ground of how to afford the greatest happiness to the units of human society during their brief transit through this sorry world. (5)

The heroine of *The Woodlanders*, Grace Melbury, is the most unfortunate victim of male abuse and social as well as legal injustice which she is forced to put up with throughout her life. She is the only daughter of George Melbury who is a rich timber merchant of Little Hintock. She has lived in the city and seen the false glamour of city life. She feels that real happiness lies not in the cultured life but in the simple ways of the woodland people. But within her, there is a conflict between her modern nerves and primitive feelings. She wavers between the two attractions and is unable to decide in favour of her love for the old fashionable ways.

The cause of Grace's tragedy lies, to a great extent, in the foolish ambition of her father, George Melbury. He has spent lots of money on Grace's education so that she may not be one of the Woodlanders. He is preoccupied with high social manners and culture since he educates Grace to be above the people in Little Hintock. The victimization of Grace begins at this point of her life, at the hands of her own father who alienates her from her family and social background by sending her to a fashionable and reputed boarding school. When Grace returns home after completing her education, Mr. Melbury takes charge of the young girl's life and affairs. Though Grace wants to marry Giles Winterborne, a sturdy young man of Little Hintock, Mr. Melbury advises her against it. He is seen here breaking his own virtuous vow to marry Grace to Giles. This was decided in order to settle a serious mistake that he had done to Giles's father by taking away Grace's mother from him in a tricky manner as he wanted to marry her himself. Feeling very guilty and miserable, Mr. Melbury had determined to atone for his sin by marrying Grace to Giles. But when the occasion to fulfil his vow comes, he feels that Grace is too good for the likes of the uneducated, poor Giles. This is made clear in his talk to his second wife.

> But since I have educated her so well, and so long, and far above the level of the daughters hereabout, it is wasting her to give her a man of no higher standing than he. (17)

Jane Lewis remarks: "Most late Victorian middle class women did not receive a good enough education to converse with their husbands as equals. They were usually educated at home, perhaps spending a few years in a private school." (1984: 125)

Mr. Melbury always brags of the education of Grace in

order to lift her up to a superior level which cannot be matched by the people of Little Hintock. But the 'fancy education' which Melbury provides for Grace, cuts her off from her former plain way of life and from her old love, Giles Winterborne. Her education is regarded by her father as an investment which will pay well in the form of a gentleman as son-in-law. In other words, Mr. Melbury thinks of his daughter as a piece of human coinage which he can use to buy higher social status. At the same time, he refuses to acknowledge that she is a woman who can decide for herself and has individuality of her own. Mr. Melbury expresses his desire to achieve a higher social status, "To sow in her heart cravings for social position was obviously his strong desire." (104)

Here, we see Mr. Melbury ruining his daughter's happiness by imposing his will on Grace, leaving no freedom to take her own decision in shaping her life. Moreover, he makes Grace promise him to break off completely with Giles Winterborne which she does with a sigh, just to please her father:

> "Promise me that you will not meet him again without my knowledge."
>
> "I never do meet him, father, either without your knowledge or with it." (105)

J.S. Mill comments: "the father had the power to dispose of his daughter in marriage at his own will and pleasure, without any regard to hers, and it was practically impossible for the girl to refuse compliance if the father persevered." (1995: 37)

Grace's response here is mixed with a sense of resignation and sympathy for Giles Winterborne. The father-daughter relationship too is also a subject of Hardy's severe criticism and condemnation. Hardy expresses it through Grace's words as to how she wished not to be her father's worldly hope. But that is not the sole cause of the tragedy. She is weak enough to be lured by social status as she does not have a clear understanding of her inner desires and of what is really good for her. In her heart, she knows the worth of Giles but is unable to decide for herself. Mary Wollstonecraft explains: "Men in their youth are prepared for professions and marriage is not considered as the grand feature in their lives, whilst women, on the contrary, have no other scheme to sharpen their faculties. To rise in the world and have the liberty of running from pleasure to pleasure, they must marry advantageously, and to this object their time is sacrificed." (1995: 68)

At this point, we see Grace being attracted by the new arrival of Dr. Fitzpiers, a young and handsome man, at Little Hintock. Grace starts thinking seriously about him. She is only looking for the social and intellectual refinement in him which she will be able to share. Mr. Melbury encourages Dr. Fitzpiers' approach to Grace and appreciates Grace's acceptance of the same. He is overwhelmed at the material prospects of this alliance when the doctor within a short period of courtship proposes to Grace:

> "I always said," continued he with a lump in his throat, "that my Grace would make a mark at her own level some day. That was why I educated her. I said to myself, I'll do it, cost what it may, though her stepmother was pretty frightened at my paying out so much money year after year. I knew it would tell in the end."
>
> "Where you've not good material to work on, such doings would be waste and vanity," I said. "But where you have that material, it is sure to be worthwhile." (185)

"Cost," "paying out so much money," "waste" and "being worthwhile" are the terms of Mr. Melbury's interest. The irony of it all is that "waste" is exactly what comes about in the end, not a material waste but a human loss, the waste of his daughter's whole life through his foolish pursuits.

Fitzpiers is portrayed as alienated from the Hintock community and an understandable character living among them. Fitzpiers's dislike for old-fashioned Woodland forms of life begins to manifest itself soon. He feels that he belongs to a different species from the people who are working in Little Hintock. He is in fact a man who can love more than one woman at once. Hardy remarks:

> He had noticed himself to be possessed by five distinct infatuations at the same time. If this were true, his differed from the highest affection as the lower orders of the animal world differ from advanced organisms, partition causing not death but a multiplied existence. (252)

His encounters with young Suke Damson which comes to the notice of Grace is brushed aside with a simple lie but his serious entanglement with Mrs. Felice Charmond, a wealthy and middle-aged widow, disturbs his married life to a great extent. Dr. Fitzpiers's desire to possess Grace is based mainly on her physical and financial assets. Hardy explains,

> Apart from his lover-like anxiety to possess her the few golden hundreds of the timber-dealer, ready to hand, formed a warm background to Grace's lovely face and went some way to remove his uneasiness at the prospect of endangering his professional and social chances by an alliance with the family of a simple countryman. (204-5)

Hardy's other emotional heroine is Felice Charmond. She is a more daring version of Eustacia Vye as Hardy is much more explicit about Felice's sexuality and desires than he ever was about Eustacia Vye. Felice Charmond is the widow of a very wealthy gentleman who was thirty years older to her. On his death, she becomes a rich landlady of certain dwellings at Hintock where her will is the law. Felice finds a diversion for her bored life at Little Hintock in Dr. Fitzpiers. Her irresistible attraction for the young and handsome doctor has serious implications on Grace Melbury's marriage. Felice's whole life depends on the emotional excitement she enjoys from her various romantic attachments as she believes: "women are always carried about like corks upon the waves of masculine desires." (228) Mary Wollstonecraft explains: "Women have seldom sufficient serious employment to silence their feelings, a round of little cares, as vain pursuits frittering away all strength of mind and organs, they become naturally only objects of sense." (1995: 85)

Yet, she makes no effort to break away from her emotional parasitism in her attachments. Hardy does not approve this aspect of her conduct. He describes her as a melodramatic temptress. She disturbs the orderly community life at Little Hintock by her role as an arrogant landlady. She evicts tenants without any mercy as soon as their leases expire and pulls down their old dwellings in order to build new ones. Yet, we notice Hardy sympathising with her as she is also a victim of intense passion and male-exploitation.

Though Felice Charmond is the seducer in her affair with Dr. Fitzpiers, at a later stage, he takes control of her feelings which she is unable to break. Even after becoming his mistress, she seems to suffer very much due to the accusations and pleadings of Mr. Melbury and Grace. Hardy is particularly insistent on this point when Grace confronts Felice Charmond. After some heated exchange of arguments, Felice whispers something in Grace's ear and instantly bursts into a violent fit of sobbing. Grace is thunder-struck at this revelation and she exclaims, "He's had you! Can it be—can it be!" (293) Subbamma Maladi indicates: "In case of debauchery, the woman is abused. She is described as a fallen woman. The man goes scot free. What is pleaded here is that there should be only one set of moral principles for both men and women." (1985: 6)

In spite of this initial shock and distress Grace has, the two women still have an alliance based on their knowledge that they both have been victims of male selfishness, deceit and abuse. Their mutual sympathy is shown in their kissing each other unconsciously and that is more important than Felice's confession. Hardy shows Fitzpiers's adulterous relationship with Felice, while marrying Grace, as male offence against two women. Thus, the alliance between Grace and Felice Charmond is a real challenge to man's mistreatment of women. Subbamma Maladi says: "Women are slaves to male domination. They are slaves to ignorance. Not only that they do not enjoy equality with men in social, economic, political and cultural sectors of life. They do not have freedom. They are slaves to their husbands and their families. Women have no individuality. They are not allowed to aspire for individual freedom." (1985: 4)

On another occasion, Suke Damson and Felice Charmond visit Dr. Fitzpiers when he is injured. Grace demonstrates helpless passivity: "You shall know all I know. Indeed, you have a perfect right to go into his bedroom; who can have better than either of you? . . . Wives all, let's enter together." (313) Here Grace's hidden jealousy and deep emotional disturbance can be seen in her open challenge to them. But she does not indulge in strong expression of her inner turbulence through protests of any kind. Her passivity and meekness are also the targets of Hardy's resentment and criticism since another woman would have fought for her husband.

Yet Hardy portrays the pain inflicted on these women as they sit at Fitzpiers's bedside, anxious of his critical state. Hardy says, "In their gestures and faces there were anxieties, affection, agony of heart—all for a man who had wronged them—had never really behaved towards either of them anyhow but selfishly." (313)

Hardy also reveals the sudden compassionate insight that overwhelms Grace as she contemplates the relationships these women have with her husband and sees it as similar to her own, without any conventionality. It is the rigid conventionality of marriage that Hardy explores in his preface to *The Woodlanders*.

In this regard Miriam Schneir quotes Susan B. Anthony saying in 1853, "I do not know whether the world is quite willing or ready to discuss the question of marriage. . . . I feel as never before, that this whole question of woman's rights turns on the pivot of the marriage relation, and, mark my word, sooner or later, it will be the topic for discussion." (1996: 23)

Mr. Melbury sees a glimmer of hope in the new divorce law. He makes all efforts to get Grace a divorce from her bondage with Fitzpiers and probably a new alliance with the faithful and devoted Giles Winterborne. Grace too, nourishes a chance coming her way to bury her unpleasant past with all the sufferings and pain she had endured.

Mr. Melbury invites Giles Winterborne once again with the prospect of marrying Grace and decides to fight his daughter's battle. He says to Giles,

> She told me only this day that she hates refinements and such like. All that my trouble and money bought for in that way is thrown away upon her quite. She'd fain be like Marty South—think o'that! the top of her ambition! perhaps she's right. Giles, she loved you under the rind: what's more she loves 'ee still—worse luck for the poor maid! (273)

Mr. Melbury keeps on blaming himself for Grace's unhappiness. He has to bear the humiliation of begging for his daughter's happiness from Mrs. Charmond and has to hear the humiliating words of Dr. Fitzpiers.

Fitzpiers's elopement with Felice to Europe is stated as ground for divorce. But a mere statement from Mr. Melbury is found not sufficient to grant Grace an annulment of her marriage and the petition is rejected. The Matrimonial Causes Act of 1887 enabled man to divorce his wife for adultery but the woman had to prove that adultery had been aggravated by other things like physical abuse and desertion. In other words, a decent woman was totally damned if she had a lover but man could do anything he liked. Hence, hope of legal freedom is dashed, as divorce laws are male-oriented. Melbury in a dejected mood informs Grace: "You are now as ever Fitzpiers's wife. I was deluded. He has not done you enough harm! You are still subject to his beck and call." (354)

S. Mukherjee and S. Ramaswamy believe that Jeremy Bentham was concerned with the marital and sexual rights of women. He argued for "the right of women to obtain divorce in case of an unhappy marriage. He dismissed the idea of an irrevocable marriage contract as 'absurd and cruel.' He writes 'to live under the constant authority of a man that one detests, is already a species of slavery,' to be constrained to receive his embraces, is a misery too great to be tolerated even in slavery itself." (1995: 22)

It is not merely that the law fails to afford simple remedies, it doesn't coincide with mature moral sense. Long before they hear of the appearance of the new divorce law, experience made Grace and her father reassess their earlier moral assumptions. When Grace hears the truth about Suke Damson's relationship with Fitzpiers, she

> was almost startled to find how little she suffered from that jealous excitement which is conventionally attributed to all wives in such circumstances. But though possessed by none of the feline wildness which it was her moral duty to experience she did not fail to suspect that she had made a frightful mistake in her marriage. Acquiescence in her father's wishes had been degradation to herself. (251)

Even the vain Mr. Melbury begins to question his previous conformity:

> He knew that a woman once given to a man for life took, as a rule, her lot as it came, and made the best of it without external interference; but for the first time he asked himself why this so generally should be done. (260)

In her preface to 1842 edition of Indiana, George Sand wrote, "The laws which still govern a woman's existence in wedlock in the family, and in society are unjust and barbarous." (1996: 26) In regard to divorce laws, Ursula Vogel says, "The husband can demand a divorce on the ground of his wife's adultery. The wife can demand a divorce, on the ground of the husband's adultery if he has lived with his concubine under the roof of the matrimonial home." (1992: 180-81)

So when the new law appears, it seems to Grace a convenient way of regularising a situation which her developing moral awareness has already approved. Shortly, she is allowed to believe that the law endorses her independent judgement.

When Mr. Melbury tells her the truth of the law, Grace has already gone far in moral emancipation to accept interpretation of the divorce laws of her status. Hence, she sets off to seek Giles's help in running away. Her progression towards liberty of the conventions has to be slowed down as she kept Giles in the rain long enough to cause his death. She explains her behaviour to Giles:

> You know what I feel for you—what I have felt for no other living man, what I shall never feel for a man again. But as I have vowed myself to somebody else than you, and cannot be released, I must behave as I do behave, and keep that vow. I am not bound to him by any divine law, after what he has done; but I have promised, and I will pay. (370)

Later, she relents and asks Giles to come inside. "Come to me, dearest! I don't mind what they say or what they think of us anymore." (374)

Giles refuses to have shelter inside and dies subsequently. Ironically, when Grace reaches her highest point of rebellion against conventional morality, she brings herself at last to conformity. Therefore, Grace in a defeated state of mind, returns to seemingly repentant Dr. Fitzpiers to start a new life with him, away from Little Hintock. Mr Melbury too accepts his defeat in this sorrowful drama of his daughter's life. He becomes speechless, having nothing to say except: "But I am hurt; I am scourged; I am astonished! In the face of this there is nothing to be said." (291)

Simone de Beauvoir remarks: "The restrictions that education and custom impose on women now limit her grasp on the universe; when the struggle to find one's place in this world is too arduous, there can be no question of getting away from it." (1988: 720)

Grace has no choice but to live with a man who, no matter how temporarily repentant, is likely to return to his old habits. Unhappy endings are hinted rather than stated. Mr. Melbury understands that this marriage is an emotional disease.

Mr. Melbury's final reflections seem fairly conclusive:

> Well—he's her husband . . . and let her take him back to her bed if she will. . . . But let her bear in mind that the woman walks and laughs somewhere at this very moment whose neck he'll be cooling next year as he does hers to-night, and as he did Felice Charmond's last year, and Suke Damson's the year afore! . . . It's a forlorn hope for her; and God knows how it will end! (439: 40)

We note that the law which should have brought deserved relief from misery turns out to be unjust and inadequate. It is certain that Hardy does not support the moral judgement implied by the double standards of law that adultery of man is insignificant. Miriam Schneir says according to Seneca Fall's Declaration, man "has created a false public sentiment by giving to the world a different code of morals for men and women, by which moral delinquencies which exclude women from society, are not only tolerated, but deemed of little account in man." (1996: 80)

Another noble character in *The Woodlanders* is Marty South. Marty's character is not drawn in detail but from the very beginning she wins our heart. The novel opens with an important incident in her life and ends with her speech. She is a person with great human potential but her aspirations are never fulfilled due to her social position and probably due to her upbringing to accept her role as a receiver. She loves Giles Winterborne secretly but never makes any outward show to let him know of it. We are filled with pity for her hopeless devotion to a man who has always been beyond her reach. When Grace Melbury tells Marty South that Giles should have married her and nobody else, Marty South says: "In all our outdoor days and years together, ma'am . . . the one thing he never spoke of to me was love; nor I to him." (400)

Marty South's devotion and endurance is expressed in the death of Giles Winterborne: "Now, my own, own love, she whispered, you are mine, and only mine; for she has forgot'ee at last, although for her you died! But I—whenever I get up I'll think of 'ee, and whenever I lie down I'll think of 'ee again." (444)

Lack of expression, evident in the Victorian women, is also a subject of disapproval to Hardy. Women should talk and express themselves openly. Women should not be treated as silent dummies or servants. We see that Grace's life is ruined because she is treated by the people closest to her, not as a person but as a commodity to be used in purchasing social status.

In *The Woodlanders*, Hardy has successfully dealt with the conventionality of marriage as an institution, the differences of sexual mores and the pain inflicted on women by men. Hardy attacks the divorce laws in a way never seen before in his earlier novels. He exposes the Victorian morality and marriage laws which crush the human spirit of ordinary souls with no hope of escape from it. Hardy also proves how the law is unjust and unequal between the spouses, besides being extremely unsympathetic to women.

Through the characterization of Grace Melbury, Hardy has effectively demonstrated how the authorities are partial in observing such a law. Dr. Fitzpiers has been living in adultery for which Mr. Melbury provides proof. Yet, the law refuses to grant Grace divorce from her husband on the grounds that he has not done enough harm to her and therefore, he has full right over her. Thus the novel ends on a note of defeat as Grace has no rights and she faces the dilemma of living with a man for whom she has no love.

Chapter Eight

Tess of the D'Urbervilles

Tess of the D'Urbervilles (1891) is the pitiable story of Tess Durbeyfield, a peasant working girl, who was seduced by Alec D'Urbervilles and the traumatic experiences she went through which culminated in retributive justice from an uncaring society. In *The Woodlanders*, Hardy attacked the stupidity of marriage laws that tied Grace to Dr. Fitzpiers despite his infidelity, but in *Tess of the D'Urbervilles*, he brought his earlier feminist views into sharper and more fashionable focus. He attacked the basic moral assumptions of the Victorian age which condemned the innocent and defenceless victim of a seducer while the actual culprit of the crime was untouched by the law.

Hardy subtitled the novel as "A Pure Woman" out of his own conviction of the essential purity of his heroine. In his preface to the novel, Hardy remarks:

> This novel being one wherein the great campaign of the heroine begins after an event in her experience which has usually been treated as fatal to her part of protagonist, or at least as the virtual ending of her enterprises and hopes, it was quite contrary to avowed conventions that the public should welcome the book, and agree with me in holding that there was something more to be said in fiction than had been said about the shaded side of a well-known catastrophe. (21)

Hardy is frank about embodying a recognizable contemporary problem in his novel. His authorial comments reveal a consistency and strength of purpose which leave no doubt that he is arguing in favour of the fallen woman. Hardy's argument is that though Tess had fallen, she should not be judged by her fall alone but by her own intentions, nature and the circumstances that compelled her to be in this position. Tess was too young when her sexual molestation took place and there was no particular intention or even romantic attachment to Alec. She had to submit herself to the will of her employer, Alec, due to her helpless situation and her ignorance about the consequences of such a relationship.

While expounding violence against women, Andrea Nye observes: "Brownmiller, in her influential *Against Our Will* placed rape at the threshold of human history as an exercise of male power over women." (1988: 97)

The controversy about *Tess of the D'Urbervilles* is about moral values. According to Hardy, Tess's purity lies in her innocence and ignorance for not having received any instructions or self-acquired knowledge on the subject from any source. Nevertheless, Hardy and his heroine attracted tremendous commendations as well as furious uproar. Erring wives wrote to him asking advice and seeking sympathy. Hardy made Tess a living entity. Hardy's challenge of the norms of Victorian age to defend the rights of women and his sympathy for them are strong proofs of his being a feminist novelist. In the preface to the first edition, Hardy wrote:

> In respect of the book's opinion and sentiments, I would ask any too genteel reader, who cannot endure to have said what everybody nowadays thinks and feels, to remember a well-worn sentence of St. Jerome's: If an offence come out of the truth, better is it that the offence come than that the truth be concealed. (19)

Here, Hardy defends his opinions forcefully. He attacks his critics logically and even invites public judgement that he deliberately treats the theme of the fallen woman by giving it a new dimension.

Tess is presented to us as an independent and a spirited

woman. Her relation with Alec was far from being romantic as it proved to be dangerous with unpredictable consequences later. Like Grace Melbury in *The Woodlanders*, a victim of her father's foolishness and vanity, Tess also was a victim of her mother, Joan Durbeyfield, whose opportunism and folly put Tess in danger in the hands of Alec D'Urberville. She rebuked Tess for failing to obtain a marriage ring from Alec. But Tess, instead, held her mother responsible for what had happened to her:

> Why didn't you tell me there was danger in menfolk? Why didn't you warn me? Ladies know what to fend hands against because they read novels that tell them of these tricks; but I never had the chance of learning in that way, and you didn't help me! (111)

Tess blamed her mother for being negligent in educating her about guarding herself. Her mother was interested only in rank and fame at the expense of her daughter's happiness. Hardy suggests that the mother should be the ultimate mentor for her daughter in such a cruel world. Therefore, Tess's mother was partly responsible for her miseries which started in Alec's beastly behaviour. In the end, the village gossip and the system of feudal life-tenancy forced Tess into accepting Alec's protection.

Tess's tragedy is also brought out by Alec D'Urberville and Angel Clare. In regard to Alec D'Urberville's role in the novel, it doesn't invite any sympathy at all. His relationship with Tess during her employment under him was strictly on master-servant basis. Tess's seduction, the birth and death of her illegitimate baby "Sorrow" brought her untold pain and sufferings. The village parson's refusal to baptize the infant before its burial made Tess do it herself. Even the burial site allotted to the newborn was in a remote corner of the graveyard usually set aside for bad characters like murderers and law-breakers. The baptism and the burial scene are highly contemptible for a progressive society and Christian tenets as per the unforgiving nature exhibited in both cases. Subbamma

Maladi explains: "Religion has condemned women to slavery from birth onwards. Society has restricted the development of her personality. Man has suppressed her talents. It is a pity that we have not realized that it is not woman alone but entire humanity that will suffer on account of oppression of women." (1985: 11)

When Angel Clare deserted Tess after marriage, Alec made another attempt to make Tess accept him. He informed her that Angel Clare would never come back to her and once again he reminded her of her little brothers and sisters who needed financial support. Being unselfish and ready to sacrifice for her family, Tess accepted Alec. At this time, Clare came to look for Tess but failed to meet her. On knowing that she had lost Clare for the second time, Tess became desperate. In addition to this, Alec's tauntings about Clare whom she still loved, provoked Tess to take the extreme step of killing him. Such action was due to frustration and the pain inflicted on her throughout the course of her life. She was forced to take the law into her own hands because there was no existing law to protect her rights. However, this invited capital punishment from the authorities regardless of the circumstances which forced Tess to commit the crime. Subbamma Maladi says: "The woman has been relegated to the second place, oppressed by society and religion and dominated by man." (1985:11)

Angel Clare with whom Tess was involved in a genuine romantic relationship was also equally responsible for Tess's tragic end. After professing unfailing love for Tess, Angel entered into a marriage with Tess, despite her unwillingness and cautious approach. Angel Clare's voluntary confession of a forty-eight hour dissipation with a strange woman was forgiven by Tess. But a similar confession from Tess about her forced sexual violation by Alec and its consequences was unacceptable to Angel Clare. He not only failed to forgive Tess and forget her past but also at that very moment, rejected her as his lawful wife. O.R. McGregor points out: "A wife might without any loss of caste . . . condone an act of adultery on the part of the husband, but a husband could not condone a similar act on the part of a wife, and for this among other reasons . . . that the adultery of the wife might be the means of palming suspicious offspring on the husband while the adultery of husband could have no such effect with regard to the wife." (1987: 20)

In spite of her earnest pleading that she was a child then, uninstructed and unaware of man-woman relationship, Angel was not at all ready to accept her: "You were more sinned against than sinning, that I admit I forgive you, but forgiveness is not all." (268) Tess quoted some cases worse than hers where the men did not mind at all. To this, Angel Clare replied: "Decrepit families imply decrepit wills, decrepit conduct. Heaven, why did you give me a handle for despising you more by informing me of your descent!" (269)

Angel Clare was referring to Tess as a descendant of the D'Urberville family. Angel Clare was unconcerned and indifferent to Tess about the consummation of their marriage. He urged Tess to say that her confession was not true but Tess stood firm by her words. We can see here that Hardy's aggressive attack is mounted against the man and the social attitudes he represents. Miriam Schneir says according to Seneca Fall's Declaration: "that the same amount of virtue, delicacy and refinement of behaviour that is required of woman in the social state, should also be required of man, and the same transgression should be visited with equal severity on both man and woman." (1996: 81)

Angel Clare is a self-consciously modern thinker who shows considerable indifference to social forms and observances. But he fails conclusively at the first test of his emancipation and proves to be deeply entrenched in convention in his attitude to women. His inconsistency demonstrates the unconscious hypocrisy of the moral codes. His change from a liberal agnostic to a puritanical moralist manifests how deep sexual prejudices are rooted even among progressive people. Angel Clare resembles Henry Knight in *A Pair of Blue Eyes* in his conventional attitude towards women. Like Angel Clare, Knight demands perfection in the woman he marries and when he discovers that Elfride has loved another man, he feels that she is an imposter. Both of them fall in love with a moral quality rather than a woman. When Elfride realizes this, she retorts by saying:

> Am I such a—mere characterless toy—as to have no attraction in me, apart from—freshness? Haven't I brains? You said—I was clever and ingenious in my thoughts, and—isn't that anything? . . . You have praised my voice, and my manner, and my accomplishments. Yet all these things together are so much rubbish because I—accidentally saw a man before you! (365)

When he learns about Elfride's overnight escape with Stephen Smith, he jumps to the conclusion that Elfride is a fallen woman and starts reacting as a representative of social morality. He is wrong about Elfride as she has spent the night quite chastely. His attitude to women has been traditional like Angel Clare:

> Elfride loved him, he knew, and he couldn't leave off loving her, but marry her he would not. If she could but be again his own Elfride—the woman she had seemed to be—but that woman was dead and buried, and he knew her no more! (389)

However, both Tess and Angel Clare were also guilty of idealizing each other and that was the reason for the failure of their marriage as much as the double moral standards and cruel social laws. Angel Clare couldn't bear the knowledge of Tess's liaison with Alec because he wanted to believe that Tess was a symbol of purity. This can be seen in his immediate reaction after Tess made her confession: "You were one person; now you are another . . . the woman I have been loving is not you." (264-65) Tess realized that Angel's response was absurd:

> I thought, Angel, that you loved me—me, my very self?. If it is I you do love, O how can it be that you look and speak so? It frightens me! Having begun to love

> you, I love you for ever—in all changes, in all disgraces, because you are yourself. I ask no more. Then how can you, O my husband, stop loving me? (264-65)

We can see that Angel Clare, an advanced and well meaning young man, was still a slave to custom and conventionality. The idealistic sexual prejudice overpowered his intelligence and tenderness. In this context, Hardy contends:

> The basic flaw in Angel is a morbid idealism—an idealism, derived from certain human institutions, certain social attitudes prevalent in his time and class, which has gone bad and become negative. (17)

However, Tess too idealized Angel Clare with whom she was in love. It was because she almost worshipped Clare, looking upto him for advice and guidance in everything, that she was unable to see his moral judgement of her as simply wrong. She accepted his decision to leave her without any protest or hesitation. Such passivity is taken as a basic flaw in the character of Tess:

> I shan't do anything, unless you order me to; and if you go away from me I shall not follow 'ee and if you never speak to me anymore I shall not ask why, unless you tell me I may. (266)

Simone de Beauvoir explains: "The woman in love who before her lover is in the position of the child before its parents is also liable to that sense of guilt she felt with them; she chooses not to revolt against him as long as she loves him, but she revolts against herself. If he loves her less than she wants him to; if she fails to engross him, to make him happy to satisfy him, all her narcissism is transformed into self-disgust, into humiliation, into hatred of herself, which drive her to self-punishment." (1988: 661-62)

Hardy asserts the dangerous state of such relationship based not on real understanding but on false, self-induced vision of the other person. Tess surrendered totally and resigned to her fate as she saw Clare infallible, almost godlike. Subbamma Maladi states: "Tradition has equated service and devotion to husband as equivalent to a higher and nobler life in world of gods. That is why women worship their husbands as 'living gods,' they sing their praise and beg for favours. In return, they receive nothing but humiliation." (1985:12)

Another factor of Tess's misfortune is that she too has absorbed the false moral code in the course of events. She is prepared to accept Clare's judgment of her even though her instincts tell her that he is a hypocrite. Hardy points out that in blaming herself for her seduction by Alec, Tess substituted a false idea of sexuality for a natural one. Hardy says that her own poor opinion of herself and her conduct is:

> based on shreds of convention, peopled by phantoms and voices antipathetic to her, was a sorry and mistaken creation of Tess's fancy—a cloud of moral hobgoblins by which she was terrified without reason. It was they that were out of harmony with the actual world, not she. (114)

Hardy blames social institution and religious establishments for Tess's sufferings as most of her miseries have been generated by her own conventional aspect and not by her innate sensitivity. Miriam Schneir refers to Elizabeth Cady Stanton saying, "Our laws and constitutions, our creeds and codes, and the custom of social life are all of masculine origin?" (1996: 28)

However, lovers in Hardy's novels find happiness only when both partners have tenderness for each other, for happiness begets happiness. Angel Clare and Tess find true happiness only when Angel learns to care for Tess and her happiness more than for his convictions and principles. In this regard, Bruce Hugman states: "The two halves of the 'perfect whole' come together for a few brief moments which seem to be as much as human frailty can bear. But they are unique and glorious moments." (1970: 60-61)

In the final analysis, Tess is portrayed as the most admirable character in the novel while the other two men in her life are depicted as the victims of false human ideals. Alec believed that he could play 'the master' to the peasant girl and Angel too believed that there was some kind of mystic purity in the lower classes. Both these characters have destructive notions as they replace individual human values with false concepts of social behaviour. Again, Angel is obsessed with the idea of feminine purity and a sceptic lacking in compassion. His ambivalent feelings are clouded by his desire to break free of his religious and social background. But such desires are seen not strong enough to withstand the confession-scene. When Tess confesses her past to him, Angel becomes too blinded by his idealistic notions. Yet, he has a genuine love for Tess which lies beneath his conscious self. The scene of Angel's sleep-walking carrying Tess across the river prepares the readers for his final realization of his true sentiments for her. However, Angel Clare is inconsistent in character. He complains about the social ordinances of marriage as constraining, when his own view of purity in his wife binds him more to the social law. He is self-alienated and one of the most complex and contradictory of Hardy's male characters.

Tess of the D'Urbervilles emphasizes also the effect of the abstract concepts about conduct. Through Angel's characterization, Hardy illustrates that life-denying ideas are extremely destructive in effect. In this novel, Hardy lifts the tale of a wronged peasant girl into the realm of tragedy. It is not only the tale of Tess Durbeyfield but also the story of sufferings and subordination of any woman. It is about a pure soul struggling against the evils of double standards and the pretentious moral and social forces. It also stands as a sustained attack on false morality with its inflexible demand for purity in women only. It reduced Tess to terrible poverty and drove her back to Alec D'Urbervilles.

In regard to the subordination and resignation of women, Simone de Beauvoir says: "This resignation inspires the patience often admired in women. They can stand physical pain much better than men: they are capable of stoical courage when circumstances demand it; lacking the male's aggressive audacity; many women distinguish themselves by their calm tenacity in passive resistance." (1988: 613)

Tess's meekness and endurance in her love for Angel Clare evoke bitter emotions which pierce the stoniest moral heart. In her last letter to Angel, she pours out her frustration and anger:

> "O why have you treated me so monstrously, Angel! I do not deserve it. I have thought it all over carefully, and I can never, never forgive you! You know that I did not intend to wrong you—why have you so wronged me? You are cruel, cruel indeed? I will try to forget you. It is all injustice I have received at your hands!"
>
> "It is quite true!" said Angel, throwing down the letter. (414)

But such response is late; it is even seen as an important change in Angel's attitude. In the end, Tess herself realizes that she was mistaken in accepting Clare's estimate of her.

Tess of the D'Urbervilles is the most outspoken of Hardy's novels in its treatment of women and sexuality. Hardy's relentless attempts to project the ills of the Victorian society and his understanding of human needs and passions are quite impressive and invaluable. Hardy's subtitling the novel as 'A Pure Woman' offended many readers and critics. Hardy had to make a number of revisions due to the critics's sensitivity to Victorian moral presumptions. However, Tess is not a New Woman but the novel which is built around her, has essential features of the New Woman fiction, disrespect for reticence about sex and calling for woman's freedom and rights. In calling Tess a 'pure' woman, Hardy challenges his readers to disagree. The novel was treated by many critics in much the same way as the New Woman fiction. It was seen as dangerous in its ideas and disagreeable in its expression of them.

Chapter Nine

Jude the Obscure

In *Jude the Obscure* (1895), Hardy begins to inspect the marital unhappiness and sexual incompatibility which social conventions refused to acknowledge and admit. The institution of marriage is attacked in *Jude the Obscure* as it is seen to be the cause of much suffering and misery.

Jude the Obscure is mainly about the shattered ideals of its two major characters—Jude Fawley and Sue Bridehead who defied the stiff Victorian moral codes regarding the conventional marriage law. In contrast to their beliefs, their attempts ended in terrible disaster not only for themselves but also for all those who were closely related to them. The agonizing experiences which the entire members of the family underwent, made Jude Fawley and Sue Bridehead see the bitter reality. They bitterly regretted the futility of fighting against the strictly laid marriage laws bringing social equality and discipline. Hardy used the oppressive marriage law as the tragic machinery of the novel to project its disastrous negative impact on the social life prevailing at that time.

Jude Fawley is portrayed as an obscure and weakwilled character which can be ascribed to his broken family background. His mother had drowned herself and father had a natural death. In addition to these traumatic experiences, there was his great aunt who openly expressed her unwillingness to take charge of his upbringing. The loneliness and helplessness had deeply affected Jude from early childhood and continued throughout his life till the very end. As a teenager, Jude wanted to learn Latin and Greek but changed to studying Gospels as they had a special appeal to him then. His ambition was to become a bishop by leading a pure and wise Christian life and to set an example by giving away a major part of his earnings in charity.

Jude's encounter with Arabella Donn at the age of nineteen changed all his plans. He came under the spell of her physical charms. They were married in a hurry and within a short time, the marriage broke off. Jude realized that their lives were ruined by the matrimonial union which is based on a temporary sexual feeling without any compatibility of their two different natures. Loneliness and despair led Jude to think of his interest in books once again and he made a move towards Christminster, the city of knowledge. Again, Jude was distracted by his cousin Sue Bridehead at Christminster. But his marital bond with Arabella stopped him from revealing his strong passion for Sue.

Jude's acquaintance with Sue Bridehead resulted in total failure of his ambitions. All his hopes of entering a university collapsed with the loss of the chance of being an ordained minister. Jude experienced defeat in love too, as Sue Bridehead decided to marry Mr. Robert Phillotson, the schoolmaster for whom she worked. But neither Jude nor Sue gave up their love for each other in spite of having their lawful marriage ties intact. Mr. Phillotson lost his profession for letting Sue live with Jude. Jude and Sue along with their children were treated as social outcasts. No job was made available to them. They were even deprived of community lodgings.

In *Jude the Obscure* Jude confronts a world which he sees indifferent to his goals. Focus on Jude's character goes on with the subject Hardy intended—the story of a young man who could not go to Oxford, his struggles and ultimate failure. In correspondence with Edmund Gosse, Hardy admits his subject has taken multi-dimensions. His novel is concerned with the "labours of a poor student to get a University degree, and secondly with the tragic issues of two bad marriages." (1962: 271)

The novel also revolves around Sue Bridehead whose role

is to project Hardy's views of marriage and unmask the deep-seated conventions which baffle Jude's hopes. Dale Kramer identifies Sue as the cause of the tragedy: "It can justly be said, Jude's choice of Sue is what dooms him." (1975: 161) Yet, Sue's portrait is Hardy's representation of what a woman should be—a woman who can decide for herself and determine her course of life but unfortunately crushed by the excessive weight of religious and social forces.

To understand Sue's character properly, it is necessary to study her relationship with various characters in the novel. Hardy speaks of Sue as "a type of woman which has always had an attraction for me." (1962: 272) Here, Hardy refers to her intellectuality and independence of thought and emotion. Like Meredith, Gissing and Moore, Hardy was deeply interested in the 'new woman' who wanted to find an identity for herself. A German reviewer remarked to Hardy: "Sue Bridehead, the heroine, was the first delineation in fiction of the woman who was coming into notice in her thousands every year—the woman of the feminist movement—the slight pale bachelor girl—the intellectualized emancipated bundle of nerves that modern conditions were producing, mainly in cities as yet, who does not recognize the necessity for most of her sex to follow marriage as a profession, and boast themselves as superior people because they are licensed to be loved on the premises." (9-10)

Sue is emancipated in the sense that she lives away from her family, works seriously and thinks brilliantly. Beneath Sue's rejection of conventions and tradition lurks a great human potential to resist the loss of identity that traditional love demands and even dictates. She shows great strength in the face of formidable pressures from Jude and Phillotson. She wants to make a life for herself without depending on any man but herself. Even after she joins Jude, she keeps her independence in whatever she did.

Sue's statements on the institutions of marriage are rational and illuminating. Hardy has made Sue the mouthpiece of his own feelings and opinions. Sue sees marriage as the most despotic kind of restriction on her freedom. She wants a relationship as close but independent as two stars revolving around each other. Hardy questions if a woman had any right to choose her husband and this is revealed through Sue's lamentation to Jude. "My bridegroom chooses me of his own will and pleasure, but I don't choose him. Somebody gives me to him, like a she-ass or a she-goat, or any other domestic animal." (203)

Hardy advocated that women should have the right to exercise their will in choosing their life partners and also in expressing their feelings. Sue's fear of marriage was only due to its coercive nature as it licensed love. Marriage as a hopelessly vulgar institution echoed by Sue frequently, showed her repugnance of being limited and restricted. Elizabeth Langland adds further: "Her feelings about marriage and sex derive from a sense of her individuality and independence, which seem to her threatened by sexual or formal commitments. She wants an identity of her own. She does not see marriage as her ultimate goal in life. She is fearful of submerging her identity in that of another or worse, of becoming a kind of chattel!" (1980: 22)

Hardy never created such an appealing character like Sue Bridehead, who searched for her own identity, so different from the conventional women. In looking for such an identity, she demanded something which men had never taken notice of and which passive women had never before questioned. Such identity can be achieved through work and financial help.

Sue Bridehead makes a contrast to Arabella Donn. Arabella always wanted somebody to rely on and this is the reason why she wanted to hook Jude. Jude was trapped by Arabella's pretended pregnancy during their courtship. When the marriage ceremony was over, she told him: "Don't take on, dear, what's done can't be undone." (71)

Arabella never had an ambition or a vision of what she should be. She conformed externally to the conventions of her time just to manipulate those conventions to her own advantage. Deep in her heart, Arabella cared little for the sanctity of marriage. She was restless and never satisfied for long and lived a licentious life. While Arabella is the earthly type of

Goddess, with a coarse kind of beauty, Sue is a compound of feelings and ideas almost devoid of sexual urgency. Mary Wollstonecraft remarks, "Women, deluded by these sentiments, sometimes, boast of their weakness, cunningly obtaining power by playing on the weakness of men; and they may well glory in their illicit sway, for, like Turkish bashaws, they have more real power than their masters: but virtue is sacrificed to temporary gratifications, and the respectability of life to the triumph of an hour." (1995: 45)

The most dominant aspect of Sue's character is her moral independence. She constantly resisted the need to conform to conventions embodied in social and religious institutions. Only after the death of her children do her guilt feelings force her to submit to such institutions. It also makes her realize the futility of fighting against the established moral norms. Hence, she decides to go back to Phillotson in order to set things right. Hardy presents Sue not as an arid case study but a living and breathing character inviting much sympathy. The outstanding difference between Sue and Arabella is that Arabella is ever willing to make concessions to the ways of the world and is insistent on gratifying her physical and social impulses. It was she who started the courtship with Jude and planned their marriage.

Another important point that Hardy stresses in the novel is that man is not entitled to force any woman, even his wife, to live with him. Hardy remarks that "a marriage should be dissolvable as soon as it becomes a cruelty to either of the parties—being then essentially and morally no marriage." (8)

In one of her letters, George Sand says, "I want divorce established in marriage. Search as I may for the remedies to sore injustice, endless misery, and the incurable passions which trouble the union of the sexes, I can see no remedy but the power of breaking and reforming the marriage bond.

Hardy makes this point clear through the characterization of Mr. Phillotson. Phillotson faced a strong disapproval of the authorities when he allowed Sue to live with Jude without the dissolution of their marriage. Arabella scolded Phillotson for letting Sue go even though the law was on his side. She reminded him that the Church discriminated against women.

> Then shall the man be guiltless; but the woman shall bear her iniquity. Men rough on us women; but we must grin and put up wi'it! (379)

Even Gillingham, Phillotson's close friend, advised him that he should tighten the reins by degrees only and he should not be too strenuous with Sue at first, as she should adjust through time. Hardy observed that women had no individuality and therefore no will to decide about their life. Therefore Hardy demonstrated that if women have to be liberated, men's attitude towards them should change. Miriam Schneir says that according to Seneca Fall's Declaration, "He allows her in Church, as well as State, but a subordinate position, claiming Apolstolic authority for her exclusion from the ministry." (1996: 79)

Sue's psychological oppression and her inability to fight it, add up the plight many women still find themselves in. Women recognize and understand their emotional involvement in an exploitative system but that doesn't mean that they can free themselves from emotional complicity in their own oppression. It is a major problem which faces the feminists that they can't make adjustment between emotional security and independence of thought. Hardy's grasp of this problem is one of the most far-sighted notions in *Jude the Obscure*.

In *Jude the Obscure*, Hardy admits the power of female sexuality Arabella won because she knew how to use her sexuality. She exploited people when they were most vulnerable. On the other hand, Sue and Jude who tried to establish a caring relationship out of wedlock were crushed and destroyed. What was ironic is that the moral conventions could accommodate Arabella but there was no place for the sexual and moral honesty of Sue and Jude. Therefore, Arabella's real counterpart in Hardy's fiction is not Sue Bridehead but in a small degree Tess Durbeyfield. Had Tess been more like Arabella, she would simply have seduced Angel Clare there and then making it impossible for him to leave her. Hardy describes Tess sexually as attractive as Arabella which makes Tess an easy victim for the amorous advances of the young Alec D'Urbervilles.

In Hardy's view, marriage is not merely a physical union but a union of ideas and tastes. Emotional and spiritual harmony between husband and wife should be the first consideration. Where there is no love and spirituality, there is no marriage. A matrimony which is based on convention and material condition to sanctify it, is the worst form of suffering in the world. In regard to Mill's view of marriage, Mukherjee and Ramaswamy remark: "The relationship between a man and a woman should be based on mutual respect and mutual love, giving due regard to one another's rights. This would make them self-reliant and self-sufficient. Unless the equal and just worth of every human being is recognized they cannot enjoy equal rights nor realize their full potential." (1995: 41)

Hardy also added that marriage is a social institution of paramount importance and therefore, it should be purged of all traces of cruelty, artificial faithfulness, and emotional frigidity which result from an ill matched union between man and woman. An easier divorce is a promise and hope for a healthier and happier life. Regarding Hardy's views on marriage, Patricia Stubbs says, "As for the existing laws governing marriage, he called them the gratuitous cause of at least half the misery of the community, and could only account for them as the product of 'a barbaric age' of gross superstition." (1979: 60)

Hardy's first marriage to Emma Gifford was not a happy one and that justifies Hardy's criticism of the marriage contract which tied people permanently even though their tastes were different. Hardy's main objection was against the irrevocability of the marriage contract to emphasize the folly of a permanent union between ill-matched couple like Jude and Arabella. Hardy remarks ironically:

> The two swore that at every other time of their lives till death took them, they would assuredly believe, feel and desire precisely as they had believed, felt and desired

> during the few preceding weeks. What was as remarkable as the undertaking itself was the fact that nobody seemed at all surprised at what they swore. (66-67)

Jude realizes his mistake later, though it is too late to stop or withdraw. Jude feels that

> their lives were . . . ruined by the fundamental error of their matrimonial union: that of having based a permanent contract on a temporary feeling which had no necessary connection with affinities that alone render a life-long comradeship tolerable. (81)

Hardy's concern about the social institutions is revealed in most of his major novels but it is in *Jude the Obscure*, that it is more pronounced. If man has created these institutions, he can easily purge them of all ills. Hardy shows it through Sue's dialogue with Phillotson: "Domestic laws should be made according to temperaments, which should be classified. If people are at all peculiar in character they have to suffer from the very rules that produce comfort in others!" (266) J.S. Mill comments: "Women cannot be expected to devote themselves to the emancipation of women, until men in considerable number are prepared to join with them in the undertaking." (1995: 99)

Due to her experience of marriage with Phillotson, Sue started seriously questioning whether marriage is a religious binding or a social contract. She was sceptical about religion as she saw marriage as a secular institution.

> If a marriage ceremony is a religious thing, it is possibly wrong, but it is only a sordid contract, based on material convenience in householding, rating, and taxing, and the inheritance of land and money by children making it necessary that the male parent should be known. (250)

She was able to convince and persuade Phillotson to agree to their separation. Her brilliant arguments changed the conventional beliefs of Phillotson. He became so enlightened that he started championing the cause of separation while talking to his friend Gillingham. He even added that he did not see why the woman and her children should not be a family unit without the man. Phillotson's decision to set Sue free was out of his kind-heartedness to free Sue as a person from a miserable and wretched contract which bound them together without any mutual understanding. Moreover, there was a vast age difference between the two.

Sue is devastatingly critical of the moral and religious orthodoxy, yet at the same time, she is emotionally bound by it. It ultimately destroys her when she is overwhelmed by the children's death. She embraces the moral dogma which she had renounced, providing her now an explanation for her sufferings. The same Christian concepts which she ridiculed in Jude earlier, drove her back to the living death with Phillotson. She attributed the death of the children to her unorthodox way of life and the intellectual framework of emancipation in her, broke down. This made Jude remark that when bitter affliction came, her intellect broke and she veered round to darkness. The final breakdown came when she mourned.

> We must conform! All the ancient wrath of the power above us has been vented upon us, His poor creatures, and we must submit. There is no choice. We must. It is no use fighting against God. (409)

Jude's struggle between Arabella Donn and Sue Bridehead who are extremely different characters is actually a battle between flesh and spirit. D.H. Lawrence considers Jude as a victim of the strongest passion known to humanity. But what is apparent is that Jude is conventional about women. Arabella called him 'a baby' as he was easily deceived by conventional appeal. Jude can be seen as a victim of conventions and traditions. Jude's complicated initial responses to Sue reveal the confusions in his attitude to woman as a friend and woman as a sexual object. Jude ponders: "If he could only get over the sense of her sex, as she seemed to be able to do so easily of his, what a comrade she would make." (184)

Jude is a victim of social institutions too, as his dream of getting educated at Christminster fails due to the lack of financial resources. To make up for the inadequacies he had suffered from, Jude joined an Artisan's Improvement Society to ensure the fulfilment of his dream of enabling poor boys to get enrolled at Christminster. He felt that his struggle will be fruitful, even though he may not himself, live to witness the success. He asserted that the University was not established for the wealthy but for people like him.

> It was my poverty and not my will that consented to be beaten. It takes two or three generations to do what I tried to do in one, and my impulses—affections—vices perhaps they should be called—were too strong not to hamper a man without advantages; who should be as cold-blooded as a fish and as selfish as a pig to have a really good chance of being one of his country's worthies. (389)

Jude happened to be immensely changed by his experiences while Sue remained just an ever-increasing accumulation of dogmas. By the time he became agnostic, Sue's own radical ideas had collapsed under the attack of conventions and traditions. Even though Jude and Sue failed to live as man and wife out of wedlock due to social pressures, their experiment was totally new to the Victorian era. Jude remarks: "Perhaps the world is not illuminated enough for such experiments as ours! who were we, to think we could act as pioneers!" (421)

Jude the Obscure received harsh criticism on account of Hardy's frank representation of the British Society of his time. Hardy was accused of introducing an unholy anti-marriage campaign. This gave him the reputation of an immoral writer intent on destroying marriage. Though Hardy was critical about marriage as an institution, he was not against monogamy. However, there were some sincere correspondents who agreed with Hardy's contention that the novel was a moral treatise, dealing with an austere subject affecting the society.

Chapter Ten

Conclusion

By the end of the nineteenth century, a group of famous novelists, mainly men, began to look sympathetically at the problems of the late nineteenth century women. George Meredith, George Gissing and Thomas Hardy and some others were in favour of the feminists. These writers often discussed the question of free union and their female characters either support themselves or live away from home. To the feminists, Thomas Hardy is one of the few Victorian male novelists who wrote in what may be called 'a female tradition.' In the beginning of his career, Hardy was greeted with the same uncertainty that had been evoked by the publication of *Adam Bede*—Was the author, a man or a woman? We should note that *Far from the Madding Crowd* was widely attributed to George Eliot.

Hardy's remarkable heroines evoked comparison with those of Charlotte Bronte, George Eliot and Jane Austen. His heroines spoke directly to women readers. For example, after the publicanon of *Tess of the D'Urbervilles*, Hardy received letters from women who hadn't dared to tell their husbands about their pre-marital experiences. A few begged to meet him privately in order that he might hear their stories.

Hardy felt that such letters came from sincere women who were really in distress. Hardy also received letters from mothers who were placing *Tess of the D'Urbervilles* into their daughter's hands to safeguard their future. There is no doubt that Hardy's treatment of the 'Woman Question' in his major novels has done the whole male and female sex a great service. In 1896, Hardy's support to the suffrage campaign was based on his belief that the women's vote will be able to break up the pernicious conventions in respect of manners, customs and the illegitimacy and the parenthood of the offspring. The feminist Clementine Black claims Hardy "as one of that brave and clear-sighted minority who have drawn a distinction between moral worth and simple chastity in women." (1892: 50) Another critic Irving Howe while assessing Hardy's work says that the novelist has a "gift for creeping intuitively into the emotional life of women and his openness to the feminine principles." (1968: 109)

Recent feminist critics remarked that women characters provide what is missing in the acquisition of masculinity and that is clearly evident in Elaine Showalter's reading of *The Mayor of Casterbridge*. Rosalind Miles says: "A woman in Hardy's hands could be made to bear a weight of suffering whose inflictions transcend the personal and move through human to sublime; he never found the same true of a male character." (1979: 38-39)

The notion of sublimity of suffering is based on the long-standing convention of the moral superiority of women. Hardy tries, through his fictional women to awaken the consciousness of society towards the sufferings and misery of women.

A thorough analysis of Hardy's major novels shows that his women characters are misused as well as abused by men. For example Troy, Alec, Wildeve and Dr. Fitzpiers misuse their women Bathsheba, Tess, Thomasin and Grace Melbury respectively. Hardy's essential representation of women consists in their challenge to customs and tradition and their resistance to reduction to a single position. He has shown his deep enthusiasm in portraying ambitious women like Bathsheba, Grace Melbury, Eustacia Vye, Mrs. Charmond and Sue who defied the norms of conventions in order to lead independent lives.

Hardy felt that it was very important to champion the cause of women because in his view, they were 'the weaker sex.' It was women who bore children and who were sacrificed to the double standards of morality. They were the ones who most likely got wrecked to pieces if anything went wrong morally. *Tess of the D'Urbervilles* and *Jude the Obscure* belong to the list of the unconventional novels that appeared in the 1890s and both end with women breaking down under the weight of repressive conditions. *Tess of the D'Urebervilles* was greatly admired by most readers who were ready to sympathize with the theme of fallen woman, a new tendency which was not familiar to the Victorian readers.

In his major novels, Hardy dealt fearlessly with unconventional themes like mistreatment of women by men, sex, marriage and divorce laws. He even staged a strong reaction against the Victorian attitude towards love and openly depicted love affairs and sexual relationships between men and women in his novels without any inhibition. The hypocritical Victorian attitude towards love and sex deluded them into believing that human life was pious. The reaction against the conventional morality gathered momentum in the last few decades of the nineteenth century due to certain factors like new social awareness and the influence of modern scientific thought. The new social awareness encouraged women's equality with men in all spheres of life. The movement for the emancipation of women, too came into vogue and in 1870 for the first time women were allowed to vote. In addition, The Married Women's Property Act in 1882 granted economic freedom to women.

However from the analysis of Hardy's major novels, it can be recorded that all of them contain irrefutable criticism of Victorian society's contemptible portrayal and treatment of women. There is ample evidence of Hardy's preoccupation with personal rustic life that he led, which has been registered with sensitivity and precision. Hardy's point of view in his earlier novels which was harshly criticized and rejected remains much the same, later in his major novels. For instance, Hardy's novels like *Under the Greenwood Tree and Far from the Madding Crowd* are based on the views he held strongly but treated mildly for fear of rejection by the publishers. His early novel, *The Poor Man and the Lady* incurred outright rejection as the Victorian society would never allow such criticism in public. However, Hardy retained his point of view and dealt with them elaborately in his later novels such as *The Return of the Native, The Mayor of Casterbridge, The Woodlanders, Tess of the D'Urbervilles* and *Jude the Obscure* despite the adverse public reaction.

Hardy was consistently interested in women. All his novels are love-stories—stories based on the endless love of women. His great compassion towards them and issues related to their lives are reflected in all his works. As his work developed, the vanities of Fancy Day and Bathsheba Everdene grew into the complex contradiction of Eustacia Vye and Sue Bridehead. By creating women characters like these, Hardy projected how the lives of women were destroyed simply because they were helplessly trapped in false morality and rigid social structures which refused to recognise them as complete human beings on par with men. Women were always at the centre of Hardy's uncompromising vision of the relationship between men and women in society. As such, his major novels project the sufferings and injustice meted out to them in a society that frustrated individual abilities and crushed their natural and human impulses. Hardy dealt with serious issues such as conventionality of marriage, mistreatment of women by men, the unequal divorce laws and lack of facilities for women's education and progress.

Hardy criticized the orthodox view of marriage but maintained that its sanctity should be kept under all circumstances. He argued that if a husband and a wife led a miserable and unhappy life, such a marriage should be dissolved, as its sanctity had no relevance at all. Mill's view of marriage is similar to Hardy's: he also felt that the relationship between man and woman in marriage should be based on mutual love and respect. Without such an understanding, they cannot enjoy equal rights, he observed. In *The Mayor of Casterbridge*, Michael Henchard felt that his wife Susan was just a burden on him and expressed his regret at having married her. Hardy remarks:

> The conversation took a high turn, as it often does on such occasions. The ruin of good men by bad wives, and, more particularly, the frustration of many a promis-

> ing youth's high aims and hopes and the extinction of his energies by an early impudent marriage, was the theme "I married at eighteen, like the fool that I was; and this is the consequence o't." He pointed at himself and the family with a wave of the hand intended to bring out the penuriousness of the exhibition. (7)

In Hardy's view, an unhappy marriage is an unbearable load of misery. He felt sympathy for men and women who were forced to live with partners they detested. He sympathizes with Sue Bridehead and Jude Fawley in *Jude the Obscure* as they were married to unsuitable and incompatible partners. Hardy recommended that existing marriage laws and social conventions should be amended if the tragedy is to be avoided.

Similarly in *The Woodlanders*, Grace Melbury is deserted by her husband Dr. Fitzpiers for a glamorous woman Mrs. Charmond but the law court doesn't permit her to divorce him. According to the new divorce laws prevailing at the time, Fitzpiers's infidelity and adultery was not harsh enough for Grace to break her marriage bond. Thus, she was doomed to continue to live as his wife. To Hardy, marriage was not just a physical union but a sharing of emotional and spiritual harmony, of ideas and tastes of the parties involved. Therefore, he argues that the institution of marriage should be cleared of all emotional coldness and all forms of cruelty which result from lack of mutual understanding between men and women. In this regard, Samuel. C. Chew says: "Marriage . . . doesn't necessarily bring unhappiness. There is tragedy enough in all conscience, but it comes from mis-mating, not from mating, from accepting as a lasting feeling what in many cases is but a momentary impulse." (1964: 132)

In *Under the Greenwood Tree*, Hardy has shown his vehement enthusiasm for Fancy Day who challenged the conventional norms of the Victorian age by taking her own decisions. She charts her destiny free from parental control especially in the choice of her good education which conforms with feminist ideals that a sound education and economic independence are the basic elements necessary to escape from the shackles of dependence and male domination. Simone de Beauvoir feels that women's horizon is closed and if women are called for concrete action, they are bold and courageous as men. But Hardy denounces Fancy Day's ficklemindedness and vanity as he sees it as an obstacle in the way of women's progress and liberation. Mary Wollstonecraft attributes women's vanity to the way they are brought up and taught to behave as dolls. She shares Hardy's view that women should not put more importance on external things but on individuality.

In *Far from the Madding Crowd*, Bathsheba Everdene is seen as a logical development of Fancy Day. In both the novels, Hardy condemns the vanity of Fancy Day and Bathsheba in an attempt to educate his heroines that vanity can't, under any circumstances, lead them to independence but will only destroy their efforts towards this goal. Hardy is all praise for Bathsheba's drift from conventionality and alluded it largely to her being a free thinking woman. What stimulated Hardy was the idea of a woman strongly individualized and totally independent. Hardy conceived *Far from the Madding Crowd* as a novel imparting moral education and meant to purge and purify Bathsheba of her vanity. In spite of its criticism, Hardy never failed to exhibit his admiration for her character. "There was a bright air and manner about her now, by which she seemed to imply that the desirability of her existence could not be questioned." (26) Bathsheba's characterization is more assertive than that of Fancy Day as she is tested to the limits of her endurance by the blows of harsh and credible events that expose her vanity and also her courage to the full.

In *The Return of the Native*, we find Eustacia Vye and Thomasin Yeobright as two characters with entirely different natures. Eustacia is a woman who defies restriction and chooses to live a free life far away from the suffocating Egdon Heath. She asserts her individuality by refusing to conform to the conventional mores and her fight and death for her self-respect marks her distinct mental make-up. In contrast to the nature of Eustacia Vye, Thomasin is a dependent woman who makes no extraordinary demands on life. Thomasin's reticence and dependence is a major hurdle for women on the road to freedom. Damon Wildeve resembles Frank Troy completely in his infidelity towards his wife Thomasin. He feels jealous when he sees Thomasin desired by someone else and that accounts for his mentality which shows that women are objects to be possessed.

Treatment of women as inessential human beings occupies the central place in *The Mayor of Casterbridge*. Michael Henchard sold his wife for five guineas and that proves our point that man never looked at woman as someone with equal dignity. We find Susan warm-hearted and passive, not sharp at all. Susan's unforgivable weakness is her passivity and simplicity which was not acceptable to Hardy though he admires endurance. Elizabeth-Jane is portrayed as a girl of sound judgement and character, totally free from vanity and fickle-mindedness. Her prudence, intelligence and general stability of character mark her as one of Hardy's endearing heroines. Lucetta, the only woman who has been involved with Henchard, is an unconventional woman who leads a free life. She is crushed out of existence by the society's disapproval of her unconventional mode of life.

In *The Mayor of Casterbridge*, Hardy suggests that proper understanding and trust between the spouses is necessary in creating a healthy society. He condemns the male-superiority exercised by Henchard when he takes advantage of Susan's simplicity. He also condemns the laws which could not protect Susan from being sold. The furmity woman's revelation of Henchard's past crime worked as an effective challenge to the authority of the patriarchal law. Hardy demonstrates that such crimes as Henchard's will never go unpunished.

In *The Woodlanders*, Grace Melbury is a victim of her husband, Dr. Fitzpiers's extramarital relationships with Suke Damson and Mrs. Charmonds. Grace pleaded for divorce on grounds of adultery but all hope of freedom from their marriage bond is dashed as the divorce laws are male-oriented. She is a victim of her father, George Melbury's preoccupation with culture and high social manners. Indeed, Grace Melbury is the most unfortunate victim of male-abuse and social as well as legal injustice which she is forced to put up with for the rest of her life.

In *The Woodlanders*, Hardy has successfully dealt with the conventionality of marriage as an institution and the mistreatment of women by men. He has fully exposed the darker side of Victorian morality and rigid marriage laws which crushed the spirit of ordinary human beings with no hope of escape from it. He has also proved how the law was unjust and unequal between the spouses, besides being unsympathetic towards women. Hardy had great sympathy for Grace Melbury who had to face the dilemma of living with a man for whom she had no love.

In *Tess of the D'Urbervilles*, Tess is a victim of man's maltreatment and double standards. The novel stands as a sustained attack on the false morality with its inflexible demand for purity in women only. Hardy's attempts to project the ills of the Victorian society and his understanding of human needs and passions are invaluable. In calling Tess a pure woman, Hardy challenges his readers to disagree. The novel which was treated in the same way as the New Woman fiction was considered to be dangerous in its ideas.

Hardy's portrayal of women characters can be classified into three groups—the vain, the ambitious and the passive. Among the vain are Fancy Day and Bathsheba. Sue Bridehead and Eustacia Vye stand for the ambitious while Susan and Tess are the passive ones. Hardy's fictional women have a sort of unshakable integrity at the bottom. In characterization, he preferred the ideal to the reality. Therefore, there is not a single heroine endowed with all his ideal qualities. The qualities Hardy highlighted in his ideal woman are purity, integrity and ambition—the woman who is independent and works for her own betterment. Elizabeth-Jane in *The Mayor of Casterbridge* comes closest to this ideal.

Thus we find that in his novels, Hardy defended women's rights despite the enormous pressures of the Victorian society of his time.

Bibliography

Primary Sources

Hardy, Thomas. 1871. *Desperate Remedies*. London: Macmillan. Reprinted 1975.

______. 1872. *Under the Greenwood Tree*. London: Penguin. Reprinted 1994.

______. 1873. *A Pair of Blue Eyes*. London: Macmillan. Reprinted 1975.

______. 1874. *Far from the Madding Crowd*. London: Penguin. Reprinted 1994.

______. 1876. *The Hand of Ethelberta*. London: Macmillan. Reprinted 1975.

______. 1878. *The Return of the Native*. New York: Oxford University Press. Reprinted 1990.

______. 1880. *The Trumpet Major*. London: Macmillan. Reprinted 1975.

______. 1881. *A Laodicean*. London: Macmillan. Reprinted 1975.

______. 1882. *Two on a Tower*. London: Macmillan. Reprinted 1975.

______. 1886. *The Mayor of Casterbridge*. London: Penguin. Reprinted 1994.

______. 1887. *The Woodlanders*. London: Penguin. Reprinted 1994.

______. 1891. *Tess of the D'Urbervillles*. New Delhi: Rupa. Reprinted 1994.

______. 1895. *Jude the Obscure*. London: Penguin. Reprinted 1994.

______. 1897. *The Well-Beloved*. London: Macmillan. Reprinted 1975.

Secondary Sources

Allen, W. 1958. *The English Novel*. London: Penguin.

Ball, D. 1986. 'Hardy's Experimental Fiction, *English*, 35, 26-36.

Banks, O. 1981. *Faces of Feminism: A Study of Feminism as a Social Movement*. New York: St. Martin Press.

Barret, A., ed. 1992. *Women's Writing in Middle English*. London:

Longman.

Black, C. 1892. "*Tess of the D'Urbervillles,*" *Illustrated London News*, 9, 50.

Blake, K. 1982. "Pure Tess; Hardy on Knowing a Woman," *Studies in English Literature*, 22, 689-706.

Boumelha, P. 1982. *Thomas Hardy and Women*. Great Britain: The Harvester Press.

Brody, M. 1983. "Mary Wollstonecraft's Sexuality and Women's Rights" in D. Spender, ed. *Feminist Theorists.*

Brown, D. 1951. *Thomas Hardy*. London: Macmillan.

Butler, St. J.L. 1978. *Thomas Hardy*. London: Cambridge University Press.

Carpenter, R. 1976. *Thomas Hardy*. London: Macmillan.

Cazamian, L. 1973. *The Social Novel in England 1830-1850*. London: Routledge & Kegan Paul.

Cecil, D. 1945. *Hardy the Novelist: An Essay in Criticism*. London: Constable.

Chew, S.C. 1964. *Thomas Hardy: Poet and Novelist*. New York: Russell and Russell.

Cixous, H. 1981. 'The Laugh of the Medusa' in *New French Feminism*, ed. M. Elaine and Isabelle de C. New York: Schocken.

Cunningham, G. 1978. *The New Woman and the Victorian Novel*. London: Macmillan.

De Beauvoir, S. 1988. *The Second Sex*. Britain: Picador.

Dollar, J.G. 1983. "The Looped Orbit of *The Mayor of Casterbridge*," *Papers on Language & Literature*, 19, 293-308.

Drabble, M. 1976. *The Genius of Thomas Hardy*. London: Weidenfled & Nicolson.

Draper, R.P. 1983. "*The Mayor of Casterbridge*," *Critical Quarterly*, 25, 57-70.

______, ed. 1975. *Thomas Hardy: The Tragic Novels*. London: Macmillan.

______, ed. 1987. *Three Pastoral Novels*. London: Macmillan.

Duffin, H.C. 1916. *Thomas Hardy: A Study of Wessex Novels*. London: Manchester University Press.

Eagleton, M., ed. 1986. *Feminist Literary Theory*. U.K: Blackwell.

______, ed. 1991. *Feminist Literary Criticism*. London: Longman.

Eagleton, T. 1982. *The Rape of Clarissa*. London: Basil Blackwell.

Elshton, J. 1981. *Public Man: Private Woman*. Oxford: Martin Robertson.

Engels, F. 1972. *The Origin of the Family, Private Property and the State*. New York: International Publishers.

Entice, A. 1979. *Thomas Hardy: Landscapes of the Mind*. London: Macmillan.

Friedan, B. 1963. *The Feminine Mystique*. U.K.: Penguin.

Gibson, J. 1996. *Thomas Hardy: A Literary Life*. London: Macmillan.

Gilman, C. 1971. *The Man-made World*. New York: Johnson Reprinters.

Gittings, R. 1978. *The Older Hardy*. London: Heinemann.

Gregor, I. 1974. *The Great Web: The Form of Hardy's Major Fiction*. London: Faber and Faber.

Gupta, P.L. 1987. "The Dramatic Element in Hardy's Fiction," *The Aligarh Journal of English Studies*, 12, 212-23.

Hands, T. 1989. *Thomas Hardy: Distracted Preacher?* London: Macmillan

Hardy, F.E. 1928. *The Early Life of Thomas Hardy*. London: Macmillan.

______. 1962. *The Life of Thomas Hardy 1840-1928*. London: Macmillan.

Hawkins, D. 1976. *Hardy: Novelist and Poet*. London: David and Charles Newton Abbot.

Horne, L. 1982. "Passion and Flood in *Far from the Madding Crowd*," *Ariel*, 13, 39-49.

Howe, I. 1968. *Thomas Hardy*. London: Weidenfeld and Nicolson .

Hugman, B. 1970. *Hardy: Tess of the D'Urbervilles*. London: Edward Arnold.

James. L. 1978. "Thomas Hardy After Fifty Years," *Southern Review*, 11, 313-24.

Johar, D. 1995. *Image of Women*. Udaipur: Shiva.

Jordan, M.E. 1982. "Thomas Hardy's *Return of the Native*, Clym Yeobright and Melancholia," *American Imago*, 39, 101-18.

Kaushik, S., ed. 1986. *Women's Oppression: Patterns and Perspectives*. New Delhi: Shakti.

Kibred, D. 1985. *Men and Feminism in Modern Literature*. London: Macmillan.

Kramer, D. 1975. *Thomas Hardy: The Forms of Tragedy*. Detroit: Wayne State University Press.

Langland, E. 1980. "A Perspective of One's Own: Thomas Hardy and the Elusive Sue Bridehead," *Studies in the Novel*, 12, 12-28.

Lerner, L., ed. 1978. *The Victorians*. London: Methuen.

Lewis, J. 1984. *Women in England: 1870-1980*. Bloomington: Indiana

University Press.

Mallet, P. 1989, "Sexual Ideology and Narrative Form in *Jude the Obscure*," *English*, 38, 211-24.

Marx, K. 1972. *A Contribution to the Critique of Political Economy*. New York: International Publishers.

McGregor, O.R. 1957. *Divorce in England*. London: Heinemann.

Miles, R. 1979. "The Women of Wessex" in A. Smith.

Millett, K. 1970. *Sexual Politics*. New York: Doubleday.

Millgate, M. 1982. *Thomas Hardy: A Biography*. London: Oxford University Press.

______. 1984. *The Life and Works of Thomas Hardy*. London: Macmillan.

Mitchell, J. 1974. *Psychoanalysis and Feminism*. New York: Vintage.

Mitchell, J. and A. Oakley, ed. 1976. *The Rights and Wrongs of Women*. Great Britain: Penguin.

Mitchell. J. 1971. *Woman's Estate*. England: Penguin.

Nye, A. 1988. *Feminist Theory and the Philosophies of Man*. New York: Routledge.

Oakley, A. 1981. *Subject Woman*. New York: Pantheon Books.

Page, N. 1977. *Thomas Hardy*. London: Routledge and Kegan Paul.

Parker, L. 1992. "Pure Woman and Tragic Heroine? Conflicting Myths in Hardy's *Tess of the D'Urbervillles*," *Studies in the Novel*, 24, 273-82.

Paterson, J. 1960. *The Making of "The Return of the Native*." U.S.A.: University of California Eng. Studies.

Pinion, F.B. 1968. *A Hardy Companion*. London: Macmillan.

______. 1978. *Art and Thought*. London: Macmillan.

Poole, A. 1981. "Men's Words and Hardy's Women," *Essays in Criticism*, 31, 328-45.

Prasad, S.P. 1976. *Thomas Hardy and D.H. Lawrence*. New Delhi: Arnold Heinemann.

Ramaswamy, S. and S. Mukherjee, ed. 1995. *John Stuart Mill: The Subjection of Women*. New Delhi: Deep & Deep.

Rich, A. 1976. *Of Woman Born: Motherhood as Experience and Institution*. New York: W.W. Norton.

Roberts, M.A. 1993. *The Novel: From its Origins to the Present Day*. London: Bloomsbury.

Romanes, G.J. 1887. "Mental Differences between Men and Women," *Nineteenth Century*, 21, 654-72.

Russell, H.D. 1979. "The Maladroit Delay: The Changing Times in

Hardy's *The Mayor of Casterbridge*," *Critical Quarterly* 21, 17-32.

Saldivar, R. 1983. "*Jude the Obscure*: Reading and the Spirit of the Law," *F.L.H.*, 50, 607-26.

Sand, G, 1996. "Indiana" in M. Schneir, ed.

Sanstroem, D. 1981, "Order and Disorder in *Jude the Obscure*," *English Literature in Transition*, 24, 6-15.

Schneir, M. 1996. *The Vintage Book of Historical Feminism*. U.K.: Vintage.

Shires, L.M. 1991. "Narrative, Gender, and Power in *Far from the Madding Crowd*," *Novel*, 24, 162-72.

Showalter, E. 1979. "The Unmanning of the Mayor of Casterbridge" in D. Kramer, ed.

______. 1997. *A Literature of their Own: British Women Novelists from Bronte to Lessing*. Princeton: Princeton University Press.

______, ed. 1986. *The New Feminist Criticism*. London: Anchor Brendon.

Sinha, A. 1981. 'Tone and Meaning in *The Mayor of Casterbridge*," *Journal of the Department of English*, 16, 7-19.

Slack, R.C. 1957. "The Text of Hardy's *Jude the Obscure*," *Nineteenth Century Fiction*, 11, 271-74.

Smart, C., ed. 1992. *Regulating Womanhood*. London & New York: Routledge.

Smith, A. 1979. *The Novels of Thomas Hardy*. London: Vision.

Spender, D., ed. 1983. *Feminist Theorists: Three Centuries of Women's Intellectual Traditions*. London: The Women's Press.

Spender, L. 1983. *Intruder on the Rights of Men: Women's unpublished Heritage*. London: Routledge and Kegan Paul.

Steele, B., ed. 1985. *D.H. Lawrence: Study of Thomas Hardy and Other Essays*. London: Cambridge University Press.

Stubbs, P. 1979. *Women and Fiction*. U.K.: Methuen.

Subbamma, M. 1985. *Women: Tradition and Culture*. New Delhi: Sterling.

Sumner, R. 1981. *Thomas Hardy: Psychological Novelist*. London: Macmillan.

Tauchert, A., ed. 1995. *Mary Wollstonecraft: A Vindication of the Rights of Woman*. London: Everyman.

Taylor, R.H. 1978. *The Personal Notebooks of Thomas Hardy*. London: Macmillan.

______ 1982. *The Neglected Hardy: Thomas Hardy's Lesser Novels.*

London: Macmillan.

Thurley, G. 1975. *The Psychology of Hardy's Novels*. Queensland: St. Lucia.

Tong, R. 1989. *Feminist Thought*. London: Unwin Hyman.

Tyagi, P. 1995. *Treatment of Love in the Novels of Thomas Hardy*. Meerut: Shalabh.

Vogel, U. 1992. "The Double Standard of Adultery in Nineteenth-Century Law" in C. Smart, *Regulating Womanhood*.

Watt, G. 1984. *The Fallen Woman in the Nineteenth Century English Novel*. London: Barnes and Noble.

White, R.J. 1974. *Thomas Hardy and History*. London: Macmillan.

Wickens, G.B. 1986. "Victorian Theories of Language and *Tess of the D'Urbervillles*," *Mosaic*, 19, 99-115.

Williams, M. 1972. *Thomas Hardy and Rural England*. London: Macmillan.

______. 1976. *A Preface to Hardy*. London: Longman.

______. 1984. *Women in the English Novel 1800-1900*. London: Macmillan.

Woolf, V. 1932. "The Novels of Thomas Hardy," *The Common Reader*, Second Series. London: The Hogarth Press.